STREET WORK

THE WAY TO POLICE OFFICER SAFETY AND SURVIVAL

Steve Albrecht

PALADIN PRESS
BOULDER, COLORADO

REPRINT PERMISSIONS

"Dog Attacks" and "Ice Methamphetamine" reprinted by permission of *Law & Order* Magazine.

"Police Nunchakus" reprinted by permission of Washington Crime News Service, *Training Aids Digest*, 1989.

"Police Restraining Devices" reprinted by permission of Petersen Publishing Company, *Firearms for Law Enforcement*.

"Working with the Feds," "9mm Safety & Handling," and "Stress Warning Signs" reprinted by permission of *Police Marksman* Magazine.

"Contact & Cover" reprinted by permission of *Police* Magazine.

"Amazingly Stupid Crooks," "Why Do We Do What We Do?", "Why Do We Put Up with You?", "Ten Funny Cop Stories," "Skinheads," "Prisoner Control," and "The Tactical Retreat" reprinted by permission of *Police & Security News*, Days Communication Inc.

Streetwork:
The Way to Police Officer Safety & Survival
by Steve Albrecht
Copyright © 1992 by Steve Albrecht

ISBN 0-87364-650-9
Printed in the United States of America

Published by Paladin Press, a division of
Paladin Enterprises, Inc., P.O. Box 1307,
Boulder, Colorado 80306, USA.
(303) 443-7250

Direct inquires and/or orders to the above address.

Contents

Acknowledgments

Police work is a profession of experience. No matter how long you work the streets, your "on-the-job" training phase never ends. You learn from your experiences, and you learn from the experiences of others. I've had the fortunate opportunity to learn from some of the best police officers in the nation. This book is a product of that opportunity.

No book on officer safety would be complete without some heartfelt thanks to some key people who led me down the path toward total officer survival.

My deepest gratitude goes to my mentor, San Diego Police Lt. John Morrison, who taught me more about patrol theory than 1,000 training officers ever could.

Also, many thanks to my partner, John Bailey, for his friendship and experience.

My gratitude to SDPD Assistant Chief Mike Rice for his support and suggestions, and to Gwen Gunn and Joe Coyle, editors extraordinaire from the award-winning San Diego Police Officers Association publication, *The Informant*, who give me a monthly forum to write about life in patrol.

As always, love to my parents, and finally, to Leslie.

Steve Albrecht
1992

To my grandfather, Jorma Pulkka (1910-1990), who could always find the good in every person and in every thing.

Introduction

The beauty of police work is that it's never the same. Few jobs offer you so many new "adventures" waiting around every corner. You can bounce from radio call to radio call and see something different every time. Where else can you find a job that gives you such power, control, and danger? Where else can you catch the baddest, maddest, and saddest people society has to offer and put them in jail?

Every time I go out into the field, I learn something about my city, my beat, the people I work for, the people I work with, my partners, and, finally, myself. Police work teaches me more about myself than any other job I've ever had. I discover my strengths, my limits, my good points, my faults, and the depth of my knowledge about life, all in the span of a patrol shift.

What I've learned about officer safety comes from the streets. No book can teach you what it's like to pull your gun and go after an armed robber. No book can make you feel what it's like to roll on the ground with a crook who wants you dead. Finally, no book can capture your thoughts and feelings after you come back to your station, check out, and head home for the night.

Books can't provide those things for you, only the streets and your experiences on the streets can do it. I am a product of the streets I police.

What follows is a collection of topics that relate to officer safety and survival—your survival as a patrol cop. This material is for you, no matter the size of the city, county, or town where you work, no matter how long or how short a time you've worn the uniform and the badge.

Experienced veteran officers can learn from this collection, just like the newest rookie. You may be familiar with some of the material and already know and use many of the officer safety techniques. Other sections may open your eyes a bit, and still others may actually change the way you conduct business in the streets.

You may not agree with everything you read. Some of the information may contradict what you've been told or taught, and some may go against your own department's policies and procedures manual. I won't mind if you question some of the things you see, but I strongly encourage you to read this entire book with an eye upon your own safety habits and practices. Take what I've written and build upon it, choosing what fits for you, personally and professionally.

Police work is a profession that demands perfection at all times. The margin for error is measured by your life. You can always improve your officer safety techniques. Being the best is how you stay alive in the field.

I've been fortunate enough to work for one of the most progressive and training-oriented police departments in the country. We are always testing new weapons, equipment, defensive tactics, and patrol procedures. These changes have not always come about because our department is so "visionary," but rather because officers have been killed or injured in our city. We have had to change the way we work to stay alive.

You can never learn enough about survival. Police work is getting more and more dangerous with each passing hour and each passing day.

Encourage your fellow officers to read this book and apply the principles to their own patrol habits. Become the local officer safety "expert" in your department by reading books, watching videos, attending courses, and practicing, preaching, and teaching the techniques and procedures that work for you. Talk about officer safety during your lineups, in the field, and in the locker room. Use every chance you get to help your fellow officers be as safe as possible at all times.

Burglary Calls: Back to the Basics

"Is there a clear unit to check an alarm at . . ."

If you've answered one of these calls, you've answered one hundred of them. A ringing alarm hardly brings a lights-and-siren response from the average police officer. If you're working alone, you probably have this conversation with yourself: "Not that place again. That stupid alarm is always going off. It's never valid, and I've gotta drive all the way across my beat to get to it."

If you're working with a partner, you both probably make similar remarks about the validity of the call or the number of times you've gone to a similar call only to walk around the building for about ten minutes, announce that every single thing checks secure, get back in your car, and drive off.

It's a common scenario. A number of factors set off burglar and panic alarms, among them: operator error, the wind, the rain, and a host of other nonburglary reasons. As we have all learned from experience, probably one call out of every ten leads to a valid burglary. So why don't we treat every burglary ringer like it may be valid?

I fall into this trap just as often as other officers. On a windy graveyard night, you may go to fifteen of these calls.

▶ 4 ◀

Get the call, go to the address, park nearby, get out of your car, walk up to the building, rattle the doors, shine your flashlight around a bit, tell the dispatcher it's secure, get back in your car, mark your journal, and drive off to the next one. Once in a great while, you may catch a guy crawling out of a window, but most times, you get there to find either nothing or a cold scene and a ransacked house. Just another "routine" night, eh?

But what happens when the call is real? What happens to your adrenal glands when you hear rustling in the bushes, or you find an open door, or you see someone leaving the scene? That's when you become a real cop. Your senses become extremely heightened. Your survival instincts sharpen, and your abilities rise to the occasion. You want to catch this guy in the worst way, and you'll use all of your training and street experience to do it.

But why wait until you sense impending danger before you "kick it into gear"? The easy answer is that it's hard to maintain that kind of intensity on every single burglary call. The professional answer is that you had better exhibit those feelings of heightened "burglar awareness" to protect yourself. Nobody wants to get shot walking around a corner, jingling keys, bouncing a flashlight beam, and turning up a loud radio to announce his or her presence. So why do we do it? Because of those nine other times when nothing happened or went wrong. But do you really want to go on living with those odds? No way.

Let's look at some of the errors even experienced officers make concerning burglary calls. Here is the stupid method:

Get the call, acknowledge it, and beat feet to the address. Whistle and daydream if you're by yourself or shoot the bull with your partner if you're working a two-officer car. Make sure the radio is on nice and loud and keep the windows rolled down to get that cool breeze. Don't look for anybody driving or walking out of the area.

Roar up the street so everyone knows you have a big engine in your car. Park about one or two houses away, get out, slam your door, hook your keys to your belt, and go up toward the location. Shine your light all over to make sure you're at the right address. Talk and joke with your partner as you walk up to the house and make sure your radio is on so you both can hear it.

Split up from your partner and walk around the building, shining your light so you don't miss anything. Make sure you stand in the lighted areas so you can see where you're going. Rattle the doorknobs, shine your light into the windows, and put your forehead up on the glass so you can see inside. Find your partner on the other side of the building, put out an "all clear," and hump it back to the car.

That's the wrong way. At best, it scares off any burglar within one thousand feet of the building. At worst, it may get you or your partner injured or killed. Why not just turn on your lights and siren to announce you're coming? Here's a better method—one that may help you catch a crook and save your hide:

Acknowledge the radio call. Head toward the call at a reasonable speed. Plan your route. Drive carefully and keep your eyes on the surrounding area. Watch for juveniles, lone males walking down the street, people carrying things or pushing shopping carts. Watch for cars driving erratically, cruising down the street with no headlights, filled with items in the back seat or trunk, etc.

Keep your radio turned down low. Keep your windows rolled up. As you get closer to the address, put your earplug in your ear and adjust your portable radio. Keep your engine speed down to a low level. Try to avoid putting out that recognizable engine "whine" that is so noticeable from police cars. (Discussions with convicted burglars reveal that they recognized the sounds of our cars even from several blocks away.) Shut your lights off near the scene—including your rear-brake light cut-off—and park far enough away from the address so you can approach quietly on foot.

How close is too close and how far away is too far away? There is no "right" answer. Let's just say that you should be far enough away to keep your car—and your approach—out of view of the alarm call address.

Get out of your car and carefully—and quietly—close your door. Secure your keys so that nothing on your body jingles at all. (Some officers carry only their car key on a separate ring, so that it can't bang against any other keys and give their position away.) Walk up to the address quietly, monitor the radio through your earpiece, and watch for sounds or movement from the area.

Plan your approach to the building. Avoid noise-making areas, like gravel, leaves, and broken glass. Stay out of the light. Avoid any position that "silhouettes" you in the light. Carry your flashlight in your nongun hand and quietly come up to the alarm address. Use hand signals to position your partner or cover unit near the building. Remember how we've all learned to cover the perimeter of a building. Use those techniques on every hot call.

Keep your flashlight off unless it's absolutely necessary to use it. Your eyes should have adjusted to the darkness as you approached. Check the outside doors quietly and slowly. Don't just grab at the knobs. Keep low and sneak past windows. Watch for blind corners and put yourself in a tactical position as much as possible. If you are jumped, it shouldn't be a surprise; you should be able to defend yourself and retain your weapon. Check your side of the perimeter and look for telltale and not so telltale signs of forced entry. If all of the doors and windows are secured but the garage door is unlocked, what does that tell you?

Officers caught a recently paroled member of a prison gang burglarizing a home. When they opened the garage door of the house, the suspect said, "Hey! What are you doing? I live here!" Not a bad trick, but those officers didn't believe him for a second, and he was quickly snapped up.

If you think you'd never fall for that old scam, consider the officers in one California town who came upon a ringing alarm and caught the "cleaning man" complete with broom and dust pan sweeping up inside the business. "It's okay. I work here. Sorry I set off the alarm," he told the officers. They waved goodbye and drove off. Mr. Clean took off his coveralls and carted away everything that wasn't nailed down. Imagine who was sued over that little judgment error.

The main thing to remember is the old saying that applies completely to police work: "There is no such thing as a routine burglary call." You may go to 100 calls a week and never experience the slightest problem. Number 101 may get you killed, if you handle it with the same lack of enthusiasm as the previous 100.

Handling burglary call after burglary call can get amazingly tedious. Accept that fact before you leave the station. More importantly, accept the fact that you need to be just as careful on a "simple" burglary call as you do with an armed robbery in progress. Use the patrol theory and officer safety tips you've learned from your training, experience, and the techniques you've picked up from other officers. Be quiet, be careful, and—above all—be safe.

Child Abuse Crimes: Case-Handling Techniques

While we always hate to think so, part of this job involves dealing with abused, neglected, or assaulted children. While many officers will admit that after a time they tend to harden themselves to the problems of most adults, this is not so with cases involving kids.

We often feel a sense of futility, going from one drug-, alcohol-, property-, or violence-related call to another, day after day. The problems rarely change, just the players. It's hard to feel any sense of accomplishment putting the same idiots in jail again and again, only to see them back on the streets.

But the problems of children are different. We have the rare chance to actually improve a bad situation. Using appropriate laws, we can remove children from dangerous, abusive homes and keep them away from violent parents, boyfriends, relatives, etc. But these events are always traumatic for everyone involved, including the children, parents, and officers themselves. Even the worst parents in the galaxy will fight to keep their children, going against all logic or reason. In these cases, I feel like saying, "Why are you suddenly so concerned about your child now that we're here? Didn't you just finish beating and abusing this poor kid?"

In the end, we can't always win every child custody battle. Legal constraints and manpower shortages at all law enforcement and social service levels make it impossible to always save the day. But there are some victories—cases in which our intervention and prosecution have taken children from an abusive relationship and put them into a healthy, loving home. Although we're limited in what we can do as patrol officers, our efforts can have a positive impact on these little people.

Keep in mind that child-related calls often fall into two categories: child molestation and child abuse/neglect/endangerment.

Child molestation cases usually involve sexual assault or sexual improprieties. Child abuse cases can run a wider range. You may get a call to meet a runaway juvenile only to find that the child has left home because he or she fears for his/her safety. Or you may be called by nervous neighbors who hear or see definite signs of abuse or neglect. Still other calls may come from teachers, nurses, or social workers who report crimes involving children they know.

While the calls may differ in nature, your response to them should center on several factors: your safety when contacting a child-abuse suspect, your ability to learn as much information as possible, your ability to document that information so other investigators or social agencies can take action, and, finally, your desire to protect and defend the rights of the child, using whatever legal means possible.

Let's look at each of these factors and focus on specific actions you can take.

Officer Safety

Family and child-related calls can be volatile and filled with unpredictable people doing extremely unpredictable things. The mother who sits crying at her kitchen table as you take her cigarette-burned baby away may be the same woman who goes after you with a butcher knife. Even terrible mothers have strong maternal instincts, so you must always protect yourself and your partner from a possible attack. If you decide to remove a child from a house, get plenty of help, including a supervisor if possible. You're inside a she-bear's cave here.

Interviewing the Child

This is by far the most challenging aspect of any child-related call. You must get all the information possible, but you can't interview a child like you would an adult. Here are some suggestions I've gathered from officers who frequently handle these calls. Taken together, they'll help you get the most from your interview:

- Start by separating the child from his or her parents. If you can, take the child out of the house to a "neutral" zone that's safe and private.
- Let them sit in your car if they want. Put them in the front seat with you and let them look at the equipment. One officer told a little girl to come and sit in her "Ghostbusters" car. The child instantly identified this as something she knew from television.
- Sit so you can relate to them at eye level. Try not to tower over them, as this just raises their anxiety level.
- Modulate your tone of voice. Speak slowly and clearly, repeating or explaining things as necessary.
- No Sgt. Joe Friday imitations. Don't use police terminology, jargon, language, or codes with these kids. It's both confusing and intimidating.
- Get a female officer if possible for little girls or a male officer for little boys. Experience tells us that same-sex interaction tends to get better results.
- Let them touch you or play with your police equipment to create a bond. This might include your whistle, keys, badge, minimag light, name tag, etc.

- Use distractors, such as badge stickers, baseball cards, pens, wristwatch, etc., to ease their minds and give them something to hold while they talk to you.
- Ask the same question several different ways.
- Let them know you trust them and they can trust you.
- Answer their questions honestly.
- If you don't know, don't lie. If you do know, tell them what will happen or what to expect so they can prepare themselves.

Writing Reports

This is the key to all follow-up activities. A sketchy report that doesn't describe the details and events surrounding the case accurately won't help the child very much. Don't make other people—detectives and social workers—do your job for you. Get as much information as you can, including:

- the ages of the children
- names, addresses, and phone numbers of witnesses
- parental history
- dates, times, and locations of police calls
- schools
- injuries
- number of police calls to the same address
- criminal history of the suspect(s)
- statements from the children.

Tell how and why you responded to the scene and what kind of action you took. Feel free to call upon your detectives during working hours for more help. Put everything you know in your report to help the appropriate people follow up later.

Protecting the Child

The law gives children certain rights of protection. We can intervene when necessary to enforce these laws. My personal philosophy says that it's always better to act on the side of caution.

Just like your gut tells you to take a borderline drunk driver in for a chemical test, your gut should also tell you when you need to take a child out of an obviously abusive home. Children can't always speak for themselves. Do what the law allows and protect these little people when you can.

Contact & Cover: Tactics for Effective Suspect Control

Too often, it's only after the deaths of police officers that we learn from our mistakes. Sadly, the police profession sometimes waits in a reactive position, changing dangerous or questionable procedures only after a tragedy. But, thankfully, when the art and science of police work decides to evolve after the loss of a fellow officer, the new techniques and officer-survival methods serve to make us all better at what we do.

From two San Diego incidents, in which three officers were gunned down by single suspects, a police procedure to save officers' lives has risen above all others to become a shining example of how to do this job safely, effectively, and with a minimum of risk. This procedure is known as "Contact & Cover." Perhaps procedure is not the correct word. Once you understand the founding principles behind Contact & Cover, you'll see it more as a way of life.

Developed in 1985 by Lt. John Morrison of the San Diego Police Department, Contact & Cover came about as a result of shootings that killed three San Diego officers in an eight-month period. From his military, SWAT, and street officer training, Morrison refined the Contact & Cover techniques into a descriptive format and began to educate street officers with it.

Contact & Cover is used any time two or more field officers contact one or more unsecured suspects. Examples might include a traffic stop, a field interview, any potentially violent call such as a family or bar fight, a warrant arrest, and any other misdemeanor or felony investigation or arrest situation.

An understanding of Contact & Cover should begin with a definition of terms.

Contact Officer

This officer initiates and conducts all the business of the contact itself. He or she has a wide variety of important duties, each of which he or she is solely responsible for. The Contact Officer talks to the suspect, writes down all of the suspect or incident information, performs all pat-downs and searches, gathers any evidence, writes all citations, and notifies the dispatcher of any relevant information. The Contact Officer is usually the officer who started the primary investigation and is responsible for the chain of custody and the evidence.

Cover Officer

This officer has significantly different duties than the Contact Officer. The Cover Officer's primary role is to protect the Contact Officer by devoting all of his or her attention to the suspect(s). While the Contact Officer deals with the suspect(s), the cover officer offers protection to the Contact Officer from a position of surveillance and control.

The cover officer watches all suspects, prevents escapes, the destruction of evidence, and, most importantly, discourages any assaults on the Contact Officer. Put simply, because the cover officer is not distracted by the "business" of the contact, he or she can concentrate on the actions and conversations of the suspect(s). The Contact Officer knows the cover officer is watching his or her back at all times.

But the cover officer's duties don't end with suspect surveillance. He or she must be ready to protect the cover officer if the suspect decides to fight. Two factors make the subject of successful intervention critical to the Contact & Cover approach:

1. More officers are killed with their own guns then ever before, and
2. 60 percent of police-officer assaults happen in front of other officers.

These facts should tell you that the likelihood of a suspect trying to assault you or kill you in front of your partner is great indeed. The cover officer must know when and how to intervene to protect the Contact Officer. In short, the cover officer must establish a "force presence."

Intervention of Cover Officer

When to intervene is usually up to the Contact Officer. If he or she can control the suspect with defensive tactics, then the cover officer should remain in position and continue to watch the suspect. Only if the Contact Officer asks for help with the suspect should the cover officer join the fight. The reasoning here is clear: the cover officer must be in a position to neutralize the suspect if he gets the Contact Officer's gun.

How many times have we heard about a suspect who takes the first officer's gun away and kills or wounds both officers because each officer is trying to wrestle the gun away? Contact & Cover effectively eliminates that scenario. If a fight unfolds and the Contact Officer is disarmed, he or she will know to move quickly out of the line of fire because the cover officer will already be in a position to shoot the suspect.

Decide Roles in Advance

For Contact & Cover to work properly, the officers must decide in advance of each call who will play which role. This isn't hard to do. Some officers working a two-man unit agree that one officer, usually the driver, will be the Contact Officer for the whole shift. Other officers trade off, switching roles each time they make a new contact. The important thing is to make the decision before you ever leave the station.

If other officers arrive on a scene that two officers are already handling, the Contact Officer will give them their own Contact & Cover instructions.

Officers working one-man units automatically become Contact Officers because they initiate their own activity. Any arriving officers will automatically take the cover officer role.

These are not hard-and-fast rules, however. One of the advantages of the Contact & Cover principle is its flexibility. In certain situations, a pair of officers may decide to switch roles during the contact. This may become necessary or beneficial if, for example, the cover officer knows the suspect from previous encounters or he or she has had some special training in areas such as narcotics, firearms, or evidence collection that the first Contact Officer may lack. The officers can easily switch roles in these cases.

Communication between Officers

Once a second unit arrives on a scene to become a cover, the Contact Officer needs to brief the cover officer on the situation. This communication is critical to the safety of both officers and should take place out of the suspect's hearing. The Contact Officer will want to tell the cover officer as much information as possible, including:

- the reason for the contact
- the suspect's crime potential

- what the Contact Officer saw or heard upon arrival
- any evidence recovered
- any information about the suspect gathered from a previous contact (i.e., criminal, mental, or violent history)
- whether or not the Contact Officer has done a pat-down
- if there are any other suspects nearby
- what the Contact Officer plans to do with the suspect.

Once the cover officer has heard this information, he or she will want to tell the Contact Officer additional information as well, including: any previous contact with the suspect, any suspicious activity the cover officer saw while driving to the scene, and any important radio information the Contact Officer missed. The cover officer will want to give a clear signal to the Contact Officer that he or she will assume the cover role.

Positioning of Officers

In high-stress situations, too many officers want to stand right next to each other. This safety-in-numbers idea is dangerous and tactically flawed. Using the Contact & Cover format, the ideal position for the cover officer is close enough to watch and talk to the Contact Officer but far enough away to get a clear front and peripheral view of the suspect and the surrounding area.

Although it's not always possible, the cover officer should stand in a position that provides some personal cover and puts the suspect at a tactical disadvantage, i.e. against a wall, facing into the sun, etc. The cover officer should choose a spot that cuts off escape routes and gives a safe background in case the suspect starts shooting.

Many officers already position themselves tactically like this during all contacts, so it's not really reinventing the wheel to follow these positioning guidelines. Just remember that as cover officer, you'll want to be in the best position possible to protect yourself and the Contact Officer from any possible assault, or to prevent the destruction of evidence or escape by the suspect.

One of the most dangerous times in any contact is when the suspect realizes that he or she is about to be arrested. A fight may erupt during or after a pat-down, when the suspect is ordered into an arrest position, or when the suspect first sees or feels the handcuffs. To prevent problems like this, Contact & Cover officers should communicate with each other prior to any movements toward the suspect.

Coded Communication

Most departments use 10 and 11 codes or penal code section numbers to speed up their radio transmissions and help officers talk in a secure manner. Take advantage of these codes to communicate safely with your contact or cover officer.

Other departments rely on specific hand signals to communicate, especially at a distance. One hand signal may mean, "I NEED IMMEDIATE HELP!" or "I HAVE A DANGEROUS SUSPECT HERE!" or "DO NOT APPROACH. COVER ME FROM YOUR CAR." Another might mean, "I ONLY NEED ROUTINE ASSISTANCE FROM YOU." Whatever hand or radio signals your department uses, make sure you know them and can use them in a stressful situation.

The Contact & Cover concept represents state-of-the-art thinking in terms of police officer survival training. Over the past several years, the idea has become a role model for federal and state law enforcement personnel and a large number of city and county police and sheriff agencies.

Summary

This widespread acceptance of the the Contact & Cover

technique should tell you one thing: *It works*. And there's no secret as to why it works: *It makes good sense*. It allows you and your cover officer to assume a complete tactical advantage, and it's easy to implement and follow.

Many officers use the Contact & Cover technique faithfully, adapting it to different situations as necessary. But for the procedures to work effectively, *all* officers have to use it all of the time. Officers who use Contact & Cover say what they like best about it is that while the one officer goes about police business with the suspect, the other officer devotes his or her complete attention to covering. That's a comforting feeling.

Here's a quick review of Contact & Cover principles:

- Officers should decide who will contact and who will cover prior to any meeting with the suspects.
- The Contact Officer conducts all of the business of the encounter.
- The cover officer is there to protect the Contact Officer by establishing a force presence.
- The Cover Officer also discourages escape attempts and prevents the destruction of evidence by assuming the best possible tactical position.
- The officers can reverse roles any time for reasons of expertise or to reinforce the safety of the contact.
- The contact and Cover Officers should use hand signals or radio code language to communicate in ways not understood by the suspect.

Many crooks have told the arresting officer later, "Yeah, I'd have tried to jump you, but I knew that other cop was watching you." Let's try to make this phrase the watchword for today's street hood. Practice Contact & Cover whenever the situation arises. Review your communication signals and use more than just the standard Code 4 if necessary. Above all, remember that Contact & Cover was designed to help you survive.

The Cord-Cuff Restraint

The cord-cuff restraint is a relatively new police restraining device used to control a suspect that may want to escape, fight, or injure himself. The cuff is made from a three-and-one-half-foot-long heavy-duty nylon strap. It has a three-inch loop on one end and a metal snap-hook on the other.

The cord-cuff restraint is used in three ways:

1. An officer can loop the cuff around the suspect's waist and attach the hook to the handcuff chain or hinge. This prevents the suspect from sliding the handcuffs around to the front of his body.
2. It can be looped separately around each of the suspect's ankles and hooked together to prevent a foot chase.
3. The cuff can be used in the hog-tie position.

The hog-tie is used for violent suspects, or for those under the influence of PCP or stimulant drugs. The suspect is placed on the ground with his hands cuffed behind him. With one officer holding the suspect down, another officer loops the cord-cuff around both of the suspect's ankles and cinches it tight. Then the officer folds the suspect's legs behind him and attaches the hook end to the handcuff hinge.

In this position, the suspect can neither fight nor escape. While this may look uncomfortable and even painful, it's used as much to protect the suspect from injury as to protect the officers from assault. This highly effective technique is usually only needed in dangerous situations that threaten the safety and welfare of both the officer and the suspect.

For those of you who now carry the cord-cuff restraint on your belt, I'm sure you have a story to tell about the first time you needed it in a pinch and it wasn't handy. I have my own stories.

One night I responded to a hot prowl burglary with three other officers. We surrounded the house and two officers went in to flush out the suspect. From my position outside, I heard a fight break out inside. I jumped over a fence and ran into the house to find the officers fighting with a screaming and kicking suspect.

We got him handcuffed but he continued to kick at us. At that point, one of us asked for a cord-cuff and got no reply. Not one cop out of the four at the scene carried a cord-cuff restraint. Being the officer with the highest ID number, I ran the one block back to my car to get mine from my briefcase in the trunk.

As you can imagine, it took some time for me to run to my car, search for the cord-cuff, and drive back to the scene. While I was doing this, the suspect (a crystal methamphetamine user) continued to fight and kick at the officers, who had to sit on him. Needless to say, we could have saved a great deal of time and effort if we had all carried the restraints.

Unfortunately, I didn't learn from this experience. Six months later, I arrested a sailor for being drunk in public. He was somewhat combative but not much of a problem once I put him in the car. While waiting for the Shore Patrol and writing out a report on the hood of my car, I looked up to see the suspect with his cuffed hands now in front of him, fishing for a match to light his cigarette. I should have kept a closer eye on him, and more importantly, I should have taken the time to wrap the cord-cuff restraint around his waist and hook it to the cuff chain.

The first example shows why you should carry the cord-cuff restraint on your belt. The second shows why you should evaluate your prisoners for their flexibility, combativeness, and ability to squirm out of the standard cuffed position. If the suspect is small or appears limber, control him by looping the cord restraint around his waist and securing it to the cuff chain.

How many officers leave their prisoners unattended at the station while conducting a records check or talking to other officers? Nearly everybody does, even in a two-officer car. The best practice is to cord-cuff every prisoner you arrest, even falling-down drunks and females. It doesn't take that long to wrap the cord around their waists and attach the hook to the cuffs. It isn't dangerous or uncomfortable for the suspect, and it may save you a lot of paperwork if he or she should happen to get the cuffs around to the front, pull back the screen, and climb out of your car. I know it sounds amazing, but it can happen if you don't use the cord-cuff as an insurance policy.

The time to learn these control maneuvers is before you have to use them on a drug-crazed psycho in the street. Practice all of the techniques until you're familiar with them. If you're not carrying the cord-cuff, start today. Have it in your back pocket or in a case on your belt. Evaluate your prisoners, and decide if the cord-cuff is necessary to prevent a fight or an escape. The cord-cuff restraint may seem like a minor piece of police equipment, but you never know when—or how much—it may come in handy.

Courts and Reports

Contrary to what you see during a typical episode of "L.A. Law," going to court is not glamorous. Thanks to the teeming numbers of cases and crooks, your time "at court" is usually spent in the officers' waiting lounge or the hallway. Not many stirring courtroom dramas or tension-filled closing arguments take place in either locale.

And these days, who even goes to court anymore? Except for the occasional moving violation ticket, most officers don't get to court very often. I can't remember the last time I went to court for a misdemeanor arrest. It's not that I'm the greatest cop in the world and make only felony pinches, it's just that most of these cases don't get past the plea-bargain level.

It should come as no surprise that many felonies also don't require trials. With crowded courts and overworked prosecutors faced with many defendants, the sheer volume dictates that a relatively small number of felony cases go to a jury trial. Usually, your average dope salesman or car thief will plead guilty at the preliminary hearing or just before the trial is put on the court calendar. Because of this, some officers rarely go to court and may be a bit apprehensive about testifying in front of a jury.

"Preparing for court," says one veteran district attorney (DA) office member, "really begins after you make the arrest and are working on the report.

"Since your reports will form the basis of your testimony, they should always be written with your court appearance in mind. Try to write your report as if you would have to explain it to a jury who was not at the scene of the arrest."

Report Writing Aids Court Testimony

Once you turn in your report and it goes to your records division, you may not see it again for several months. Be aware that your report must truly paint a "word picture" that tells what you saw, what you heard, and what you did. Keep in mind that your report will face heavy scrutiny by prosecutors, investigators, and defense attorneys. If you document the entire sequence of events leading up to the arrest, you'll be able to properly recall that information if you have to testify in court.

The old rule that says, "There's always time to do it right the first time," is especially true about writing police reports. If you think a particular piece of information is important to the case, include it in your report. It can be embarrassing to explain in court why you failed to document a crucial part of the case at the time it happened.

A veteran detective supervisor adds that "you must pay close attention to the sequence of events and the statements made by everyone involved in the case. Separate your opinions and impressions from the facts. Your opinions and impressions are valid and important, but they must be labeled as such. Don't be afraid to document them in your report by noting, 'Based on what I saw, I formed the opinion that . . .' or 'My impression was that . . .'"

Careful documentation of the witness, victim, and suspect statements is also critical to the success of your case in court. When putting statements into your report, make a clear distinction between quotes and paraphrases. Use quotation marks to label exact quotations from the participants. If you aren't going to quote complete conversations, use a phrase like "The witness told me in essence that . . ."

Your report should serve as a history of the conversations that took place. Clarify whether you tape-recorded any conversations or not, and if you made notes of any conversations at the scene or away from the scene.

Contact the DA's Office

Once you complete your report and you receive a subpoena for the case, make sure you contact the DA's Office or the appropriate city attorney assigned to it. "This is especially true with felony cases," says a supervising DA, adding that although the pretrial meeting with the prosecutor may be brief, it's critical to the success of the case.

(I'm reminded of the old story involving the city attorney's office. Advised on their subpoenas to call prior to the court date, many rookie officers have asked to speak to "City Attorney Noca," only to hear the receptionist tell them that "NOCA" actually stands for "No City Attorney Assigned.")

Many deputy district attorneys (DDAs) reiterate the importance of a quality report. "Make sure you've picked up a copy of your report," says one, "and reviewed it thoroughly *before* you get to court. Don't rely on the prosecutors to give you a copy of your own work. Also, don't make them fish for information about the case. Tell them what you know about it and make sure they know of any possible surprises. If something about the case is bad, weak, or tricky, make sure you discuss it with the prosecutors in advance, so they can address it before the trial."

Courtroom Demeanor

All DDAs stress the importance of proper courtroom demeanor, including a professional appearance. "Juries want to see the police as 'the good guys,' so your attitude and appearance can play a large part in their desire to believe in you," says one.

Honesty

Complete honesty on the witness stand is of the utmost importance. No matter what happens or how the case turns out, you must tell the truth. Your job is to be as candid and ethical as possible. No arrest is worth stretching the truth just to get a conviction. Tell the jury what you did and why you did it. Don't try to help the prosecutors (or the defense) by offering more information than they ask for. Conversely, if you don't know the answer to a question, say so.

Plain Talk

One of the keys to your success on the witness stand is to "talk and act like a regular person." This means that you should use plain English to express yourself, avoiding police codes and jargon at all times. Don't say, "The perpetrator exited the vehicle and proceeded southbound." The jury wants to see you as one of them, not some elite "supercop."

One veteran DDA says, "You should think in terms of 'teaching' the jury what you know about the case. Tell them what they need to know to understand everything you saw and did." He adds that above all, officers should see the activities in the courtroom as just a portion of the whole criminal justice process. "Solving the case and making the arrest is only a part of your duties. Prosecuting and convicting these people is the final and most important part."

Summary

Write solid, thorough reports, review them carefully before you reach the witness stand, and tell the judge and jury exactly what you saw and did. By going to court, you get the unique chance to see the positive results of all your hard work on the streets.

Cross-Fire
Cautions

A cross-fire situation is an easy position to put ourselves into simply because we contact so many people everyday, and most of these stops and Field Interviews (FI) usually go by the book. How many times have you stood behind a suspect while your partner wrote out a citation (or "cite") or an FI? What if the suspect pulled a gun and started shooting? If you or your partner had to return fire, you both could miss and hit each other.

I'll admit I fall into this habit of standing behind a questionable suspect when I think I may need to put my arm around his neck. But the potential for cross fire in this situation is a problem. We should stand off to the side—at the suspect's shoulder—to eliminate this tactical error.

How many times have you walked through an alley several yards ahead of your partner? What if a suspect jumped out of a doorway with a gun? You could be in your partner's line of fire if he or she draws first.

High-risk vehicle stops and other felony arrests also present cross-fire problems. In the haste and excitement of the moment, too many officers step in front of each other's guns to make the arrest. This is particularly true during high-risk vehicle stops, during which you'll often see ten cops pointing guns in all directions.

I remember being involved with a jewelry store robbery case with multiple suspects. As I brought one of the suspects toward me, another officer stepped in front of me and snapped my cuffs on the suspect. The officer didn't seem to notice that the barrel of my gun almost brushed against the back of his head as he went past me. He was that close and didn't even see it. This type of funnel vision can cause problems if shots are fired.

Cross-fire safety starts with good common sense. Be aware of your position, your partner's position, and the position of other officers. Always try to foresee the worst-case scenario so you'll know where to stand and especially where not to stand.

The Deadly Umbrella and Other Dangerous Weapons

It should come as little surprise that human beings have always been an inventive lot. From the earliest existence of man in caves until the advent of today's pager watch, we've always known how to make things.

Primal man discovered how to sharpen certain stones into cutting weapons. Ironically, you can see this type of behavior in our prisons and jails today. What does that tell you about who dwells inside these places? You can count on them to turn whatever they can lay their hands on into weapons.

At a seminar I attended on contraband and homemade weapons, the instructor covered an entire eight-foot table with examples of improvised weapons and their hiding places. What follows is a list of these little goodies. Be aware of a crook's potential to make a weapon out of anything. You may never see these items, or you may run across one during a pat-down tomorrow. Search carefully and keep an open mind about weapons. Nothing is ever as harmless as it looks.

- Belt-buckle gun

- Belt-buckle knife
- Boot/pants clip knives
- Brass knuckles around a knife handle
- Briefcase with a gun and a firing spring clipped inside
- Briefcase with a gun built into the handle
- Carrying bag with Kevlar vest panel inside
- Cigarette lighter with knife inside
- "Distraction" two-piece key rings—drop one item on the floor; stab with the other
- Fake oil cans with guns, knives, and dope inside
- Fake pager with a .22 derringer inside
- Fanny pack with gun inside
- Firing ballistic knife
- Gravity knives that spring open
- Hollowed-out books with guns, knives, and dope inside
- Jockstrap revolver holster
- Key-ring knife
- Knife comb replaced with a switchblade knife
- Knife inside man's tie
- Knives on lanyards
- Kubotan with a metal ball on the end
- Kubotan with throwing darts inside
- Lipstick tube knife
- Mascara tube knife
- Nail-polish brush replaced with roofing nail
- Pen-and-pencil-set knives
- Plastic "hooker" or bangle bracelets with knives or nails inside
- Purse with slash compartments for gun

- Razor-blade box cutters
- Razor blade taped to a credit card or driver's license
- Religious jewelry/cross knife
- Sharpened keys
- Sharpened metal or plastic ice scraper
- Sharpened side edge or sharpened points on sunglasses
- Small gun inside man's tie
- Squirting cigarettes with ammonia or acid inside
- Sword cane
- Wallet guns
- Wallet knives
- Woman's clutch bag with a gun activated by a wrist strap.

If you want more information about these and other dangerous weapons, pick up a copy of *Street Weapons* by Edward J. Nowicki and Dennis Ramsey. This well-researched and finely detailed book is available from Performance Dimensions Publishing, P.O. Box 502, Powers Lake, WI 53159-0502.

A number of military supply catalogs hit my desk every few months, and I like to page through them to see the new weapons. These glossy, four-color booklets display some nasty-looking hideout weapons many police officers have seen in the field—pen knives, pen picks, belt knives, credit-card knives, and a variety of equally sharp, dangerous toys that may not be so familiar.

One item like this is the "Protection Sword Umbrella." What follows is some of the ad copy from the full-page advertisement.

> *Our unique folding Sword Umbrella keeps you safe from showers or a surprise attack! In the event of an assault, you can instantly draw a ten-inch surgical stainless-steel blade hidden inside the telescoping*

umbrella shaft. You become the master of the situation quickly and effectively.

This blade . . . has a 2-1/2" long precision ground, tapered point specifically designed for deep penetration. We drove one through a steel helmet with no deformation to the blade or point. It can flex up to 30 degrees and never break . . .

The sight of this deadly sword appearing in your hand, as if by magic, is enough to strike fear in the heart of any would-be mugger. It gives you peace of mind to know it's always ready when you need it.

The locking system is designed so well, it's practically impossible for anyone to figure out how to unlock the blade if they don't know the secret, even if they know it's a sword umbrella!

Fits your hand like the old "plow handle" grip on a Colt pistol to give you powerful thrusting action. Since this umbrella is lightweight—only 18 ounces—you can easily carry it in your briefcase, glove compartment, trench-coat pocket, or comfortably in your hand.

Whew! That's quite a description for a seemingly harmless little "self-protection" device. This object of beauty sells for about $75 and includes an attractive carrying sleeve and a detailed instruction manual. I think the key words and phrases in the ad copy are "surprise attack," "hidden blade," "designed for deep penetration," "appearing in your hand as if by magic," "impossible to figure out how to unlock," and "you can easily carry it."

As you can see by what you read and what your gut instinct tells you, this rain-guarding weapon is also a ten-inch, concealed ice pick. The biggest problem I see is that if you do come across someone armed with this weapon, you may not know it. Since the manufacturer tried to make the hidden blade design so clever, you may have difficulty opening the thing to find out.

This umbrella looks like any other ordinary black nylon number carried by business people or street gangsters. If it's not raining and someone is carrying one of these, I'd certainly want to know why. In case you start to feel a bit complacent in the field and don't think you want to be part of the "umbrella police," consider this: a ten-inch steel blade will cut through your bulletproof vest like it's going through butter.

Dog Attacks: Prevention and Control

"Diplomacy is the art of saying, 'Nice doggie,' until you can find a rock."

—*Wynn Catlin*

If you saw the movie *Raising Arizona*, you'll remember the Doberman pinscher scene. In it, actor Nicolas Cage is on the lam from the cops for a convenience-store robbery he has just pulled. He cuts through a dark yard and heads for the back fence. As he begins to climb over, he hears a jingling sound behind him. He turns to see a full-grown Doberman moving towards him at Mach 10 speed. The dog leaps for his throat. Cage flattens himself against the fence and pulls his head back in the nick of time as the dog jerks against the end of his chain. Cage gets away and the chase continues.

It's a funny scene—but only in the movies—and since art has a nasty habit of imitating life, an attacking dog can offer some real tactical problems for you in the field.

Mean-spirited "attack" dogs are often used to guard dope houses from other crooks and cops. Most dopers use pit bulls, Dobermans, and rottweilers, inbred for their fierceness and well-known for loyalty to their owners. But any dog can bite you—big or small, attack-trained or not, junkyard or pedigree. According to the Humane Society, cocker spaniels and chows bite the most. Remember, a chance encounter with any aggressive dog could put you on the disabled list for life.

I'll bet that every officer in this country can tell a story that begins with, "I remember the time we went to this house, and this damned dog came out and . . ." Dogs are like cars; nearly everybody has one.

Remember the female Los Angeles County Animal Control officer bit by the pit bull on national TV? As news cameras rolled, the dog's owner let it out of the house with a command to attack the officer. With no gun to protect her, she received a serious arm wound before other animal-control people saved her.

Some officers have had the misfortune to be bitten by a dog, and still others have had to kill a dog, usually in front of a flock of not-so-friendly witnesses. Remember that shooting a dog is not unlike shooting a human being because of the emotional involvement of everyone concerned. Tempers and emotions can run high at dog-shooting scenes. The same people who know why you shot a guy coming at you with a crowbar ask how you can shoot that "nice little dog" that's about to sink its teeth into your leg.

I remember looking for two crooks who had stolen a car. We followed them into a residential area and began to check the yards. My partner chased them through a backyard where a German shepherd was waiting. The dog bit him on the thigh before he shot it, literally, off of his leg. Of course, the fine symbols of humanity at the scene (several parolees, meth users, and assorted cave dwellers) could only complain about the death of the poor "defenseless" animal with the razor-sharp fangs.

My partner ended up in the back of an ambulance headed to a local hospital. He suffered through shots, stitches, antibiotics, ripped pants, and the interminable wait for the dead dog to pass the rabies quarantine period. Animal control officers told us later that they had seized the animal several times for terrorizing other dogs and people in the neighborhood.

The old saying "If it's between me and you, it's gonna be me" must certainly apply to attacking dogs. Little Johnnie can always get another family pet. You can't always fix what's been bitten on your body. Rabies shots, injected into the stomach, are painful and numerous. You're the one who will suffer through the bite, the stitches at the hospital, and the assortment of shots if that "nice doggie" gets to you first.

Assessing the Threat Potential

Let's look at some ways to identify the threat potential of a dog. Animals display noticeable characteristics when they feel afraid, threatened, or angry. Just as you "read" people on the street, you can read dogs by their movements, sounds, and stances.

But as with any potentially dangerous encounter, there are no hard-and-fast rules. No two dogs are ever the same, and signs exhibited by one dog that say, "I'm friendly. What about you?" may mean, "I'm ready to bite. Stay away!" for another.

Look for Evidence of a Dog

According to a kennelmaster at the Humane Society, you must start thinking about the presence of an attacking dog as soon as you approach any scene. Always look around the yard before going to the door of a residence. Watch for telltale signs, including dog excrement on the ground, a water or food dish, a collection of pet toys and bones—even the presence of a fence can indicate a dog. If you see evidence of a dog, stay alert for its approach. The dog may be hiding under the porch or waiting in some nearby bushes for you to pass its position.

One California State Humane officer suggests lightly kicking the fence gate before you enter any yard. This will rouse the dog to come around so you can evaluate its aggression level. Of course, in most cases, the dog will smell and hear you coming long before you get to the gate. But if it's hiding, the slightest noise will usually bring it out.

Tail Wagging—Friendly or Not?

Tail wagging, warn Humane officers, can offer you only limited information about the dog's threat level. Most dogs who wag their tails when you approach are doing it because they're "feeling you out." Tail wagging may mean friendliness in some dogs, but I remember seeing a pit bull wag its tail like a windmill as it bit the dickens out of somebody's arm.

Is His Bark Worse Than His Bite?

Barking also may or may not tell you how the dog feels about your presence. Some dogs bark without biting, some dogs bark and then bite, and some dogs, like rottweilers, don't make a sound before they attack. Barking may not mean the dog will bite, but growling, especially if the dog is moving around you, is a good indication of immediate trouble.

Avoiding Eye Contact

Humane officers recommend that you *do not* make strict eye contact with any dog, as the animal may feel you're challenging it. Remember, if you come into a dog's yard, you're treading upon its property. Dogs feel very protective of their territory. Nevertheless, while you should avoid heavy eye contact with a dog, never take your eyes off of it as you move.

If possible, approach the dog slowly, coming in at an angle instead of head-on. If you can slowly circle around a dog, it tends to calm or confuse the animal, and this can improve your advantage. If the dog comes slowly toward you, try to "stand low" so as not to intimidate it.

Sniffing Out Trouble

Many dogs like to sniff out their foes, so it's best not to carry anything in your hands if you can help it. If the dog acts as if it wants to sniff your hand, stand still. If it tries to sniff and nuzzle against you, this is usually a good sign, but you should still be on your guard.

Warning Signs of an Attack

Just like street folks, dogs exhibit definite warning signs that indicate an impending battle. If you see the animal turn slowly around you or crouch nearby, growling in low tones, look out. When a dog turns its face away from you, it usually means the animal is afraid, which is not good. If the dog's ears are pulled back and it hunches down as it barks or growls, prepare for an attack.

Most dogs will charge before they attack, so you may be able to turn them away with a loud command of "NO!" or "SIT!" Again, there is no guarantee this tactic will work, but many nonattack dogs will back down when they hear your voice commanding them. But as one veteran cop pointed out, "Dogs don't care about your badge, gun, or command presence."

What to Do if Attacked

Defending yourself against an attacking dog is not easy. You have to make split-second decisions or risk a serious injury. Before you react, you must consider the location of the attack, your footing, the time of day, the lighting conditions, and your proximity to other suspects or innocent bystanders. You have to decide whether to use your gun or some other weapon to disable the animal. If you shoot, can you hit the dog in a fatal area, and if you miss, where will the stray round land?

Another problem is that, thanks to thousands of years of evolution, the dog's body has evolved into an efficient fighting machine. A large dog's bony, curved head may deflect or absorb your bullets without stopping the fight. A dog's brain is small when compared to (most) humans', and it's hard to hit with a poorly placed shot. In big dogs, the carotid arteries are located deep within the neck muscles. This makes them hard to reach for other throat-biting dogs, but hard to reach for you as well. The veins closer to the surface of a dog's skin may not bleed enough to save you from receiving a serious bite.

A dog's heart is also buried under a stout set of ribs. In large dogs, you would need to use a knife with at least a six-inch blade to reach its heart. Even then, you'll need to use surgical precision to place the knife blade in the right spot.

Use of Force Rule

As with any violent encounter, remember that the use of force sliding scale applies to dogs as well as humans. To counter an aggressive dog, try using loud verbal commands first, then avoid the dog and call for animal control people to restrain it. If danger is imminent, try kicking, punching, or striking the dog with your baton, flashlight, or any heavy object you can get your hands on. If you cannot defend yourself and you risk great bodily injury, use your firearm, but only after exhausting all possibilities concerning your safety and the safety of others.

If You Are Unarmed

If you find yourself without your gun, you'll have to improvise quickly to protect yourself. Shoving something large into the dog's mouth—other than a part of your anatomy—may slow it down. A flashlight, Mace can, or radio might work well enough to give you time to get away.

Remember that most dogs don't blink when you zap them with your trusty Mace. It may work if you really soak their eyeballs, but if you don't score a direct hit, you'll probably just irritate them.

Dogs have certain areas of vulnerability on their bodies. Like humans, the eyes, nose, ears, and fleshy jowls behind the neck are sensitive places to a dog. Yes, even the—for lack of a better phrase—reproductive organs on a male dog are susceptible to a crippling punch or kick.

Many experts suggest that if the dog has succeeded in biting you, the best thing to do is to lift it off its feet. Grasping the fleshy area behind the neck and jerking the animal into the air will disorient it and allow you to pry the jaws off your body. In a worst-case scenario, you may have to batter the dog against a nearby wall to get it to release you. We're talking about survival here. How would you like to bleed to death at the scene because you failed to respond with controlled aggression against an attacker (animal or otherwise)?

Other defensive moves against an attacking dog include a sharp blow to the top of the dog's nose, especially in long-snouted animals like German shepherds and Dobermans.

If You Have to Shoot

Shooting a dog should be your last resort, but if you have to shoot, make the bullet count. Some dogs, like pit bulls, have a head like a shovel blade, and with their solid, bony skulls, a poor shot will barely make a dent.

The rule of thumb when shooting to stop an attacking dog is to aim for the crossing point between the dog's ears and eyes. Other tactics include shooting into the dog's open mouth at an upward angle, so the bullet penetrates the soft roof of its mouth.

There are no simple solutions for stopping a determined pit bull. One California State Humane officer says that the best place to shoot an angry pit bull is "everywhere." Just like a PCP-user that takes a revolver-full of lead and keeps coming, a well-trained pit bull will not respond to pain until its brain and heart finally shut down.

Edged-Weapon Attacks: Video Training

Recent statistics tell us the chances of your coming up against a suspect armed with a knife are definitely increasing. Consider that we've seen a 92-percent rise in edged-weapon attacks against police officers since 1978. Think about the fact that more officers are knifed during disturbance calls than during all other knife-injury calls combined.

Experts blame this rise in knife or edged-weapon assaults on a number of factors, including a tendency for the courts to treat knife-wielding suspects as less threatening than gun users; a rise in the number of immigrants from Latin, Asian, and other cultures where knives are widely respected as fighting weapons; and the fact that more crooks are turning to edged weapons because they are easy to conceal, don't jam or require cleaning, and make no noise.

To date, defensive training for knife assaults has been sketchy at best, or totally wrong at worst. To deal with this training gap, the people at Calibre Press, publishers of the well-known *The Tactical Edge* and *Street Survival* books, created *Surviving Edged Weapons*, a videotape that addresses knife and other edged-weapon problems.

The producers and cofounders of Calibre Press, Dennis Anderson and Charles Remsberg, went to great lengths to include footage of realistic edged weapons injuries, deaths, and other significant police officer training data.

For eighty-five minutes, the video takes you through a number of realistic scenarios where officers encounter suspects having edged weapons. These scenes also point out grave tactical errors that ended in death or serious injury to the officers.

One important highlight of the movie is a harrowing series of interviews with nine police officers who survived knife attacks. They all said they never saw the knife, and the attack happened much too quickly for them to respond.

In some cases, the knives even went right through the officers' body armor. In fact, one demonstration has a "Tanto" knife going through a car door like it was paper.

Several grisly morgue photos are interspaced throughout the tape to illustrate the stopping power of a typical edged weapon. You'll see photos of people stabbed or slashed with razors, scissors, forks, screwdrivers, twin-handled balisong "butterfly" knives, hunting arrows, dirks, daggers, and knives of all shapes and sizes.

The photos illustrate one important point: most edged-weapon attacks involve multiple slashes and stabs, not just one wound. The suspect doesn't just go after you once, but several times, until you are badly cut or dead.

You'll also see actual footage of prison inmates practicing knife assaults that begin from the typical wall search. The tape displays a variety of homemade prison knives and even spears confiscated during cell searches.

Another highlight of the video features two top combat knife experts showing their deadly and amazingly quick fighting techniques. These demonstrations show how the standard response to a knife attack, "I'll just pull out my gun and shoot the guy," is not a realistic answer. The video offers more practical suggestions to combat a knife attack. It teaches firearm, baton, and hand-to-hand techniques that offer better protection than the standard "put your hands up and block it" move.

Other lessons include a surprising look at the twenty-one-foot "reactionary gap," the distance you need to safely protect yourself from a knife attack; some effective search techniques; and even some medical tips to help you survive a stabbing until help arrives.

Surviving Edged Weapons is an informative, low-priced, action-packed video. For ordering information, contact Calibre Press, 666 Dundee Road, Suite 1607, Northbrook, IL 60062-2760.

Exercise and Live: Serious Motivation for the Patrol Officer

"There are convicts sitting in state prisons pumping iron all day long. They lift weights and they think about getting out and they think about you. If you're not ready and in shape, they're gonna tear your head off and throw it in the dirt."

This quote was part of my introduction to the rigors of law enforcement. While attending the graduation of a friend from the California Highway Patrol Academy, I heard this speech given to a class of cadets during the first day of physical training. The instructor paced about the gym floor and offered some practical advice to the wide-eyed recruits. The idea behind that speech never left me. Aggressive, muscular convicts don't do much for my peace of mind.

Police fitness, or the lack of it, is a frequent topic in law enforcement magazines. A number of authors have written a great number of words urging cops to exercise, build muscular strength, lose fat, and improve their cardiovascular stamina.

Too often it falls on deaf ears because it's always easier said than done. Once you start an exercise program, it seems like the excuses rise in accordance with the pain level. "No pain, no gain" turns into "This hurts. I'm quitting."

I bet that on New Year's Day, scores of officers made a determined resolution to "lose a few pounds and really get in shape this year." But I'd also be willing to bet that a large majority of them started an overly ambitious exercise program that drove them to quit after a few weeks. Why? Too much, too soon.

Whoever said all things in moderation wasn't kidding. Starting a fitness program is like being a child: first you crawl, then you walk, then you run. As a beginner, putting yourself through a torturous workout is the quickest way to lose your enthusiasm for exercise.

If you've ever been on an exercise program but fell off the wagon because of various excuses, it's time to dust yourself off and get back to work. But this time, remember to start slowly and build your workouts over a proper period of time. Fitness experts say that a 10-percent increase in your current level every two to four weeks is a good rule of thumb. As an example, if you can run for twenty minutes, three times per week, go up to twenty-two minutes when you feel ready. To avoid the pain and injuries that cause you to quit, you need to progress gradually. It took a few months to put on that beer gut. It'll take a few months to remove it.

One good thing about physical fitness is that one size doesn't have to fit all. When you can choose something you like, you're more apt to stick with it. Just make sure you get a proper mix of upper- and lower-body muscle toning and include at least three sessions of twenty- to thirty-minute cardiovascular workouts per week.

Some cops love to lift weights but hate to run. Some officers love to run but can't stand to be in a weight room. Just pick what you like to do.

If you dislike running but need the cardiovascular work, try riding a stationary bike at least three times per week. If you don't care for serious weight-lifting sessions, supplement your running or bicycling workouts with light dumb-bell sets, calisthenics, or Nautilus machine exercises.

If you're lucky enough to work at a police station with an exercise room, use it. If you don't want to exercise at work, you can find a number of bargains at area gyms. Some fitness centers in your town may offer law-enforcement discounts. If you bring a partner along to sign up, both of you may get a bargain rate.

Remember that you don't necessarily need to work out at a gym to keep in shape. Use your body as a weight-lifting machine. Start with push-ups, sit-ups, dips, and pull-ups. If you don't think these exercises will improve your build, take a look at a fairly decent football player named Herschel Walker. He rarely lifts weights, but he gained enormous strength through sets of push-ups, sit-ups, and pull-ups.

Start slow, stick with something you like, and work to improve yourself. No belly-aching allowed. I've heard and used all of the anti-exercise excuses: it's too hot, it's too cold, I'm tired from graveyard shift, I'm tired from court, I'm sick, I'm hungry, I've got to get up early tomorrow, I went to bed late last night, my back hurts, I've got a hangover, etc. If it's possible, I've thought of it and tried to use it to avoid a training session.

Someone once said there are only two things that should stop you from working out at least three times a week: a death in the family or a high fever. Enough said? But you can take a more positive approach, which leads to the most important reason to get fit and stay fit: the enemy who fills those streets and jails where you work is certainly interested in fitness. You can be sure those "muscleheads" inside our county jails and state prisons are not missing too many workouts because of their active social schedules. Every day you miss is another day they gain ground on you. Think about it.

Most of these solid penal citizens get three starchy meals a day, plenty of time to lift taxpayer-issued weights, ten hours of sleep, and all the fresh air and sunshine they can stand.

Exercising is not always going to be fun. On certain days it will just be a chore, but that's understandable. As long as you keep plugging away, you'll succeed in whatever program you choose. The benefits are obvious.

Consider this important and deadly serious message: every day you don't do something to strengthen your body is another day wasted. And another day wasted is one more day for some crook to get ahead of you.

A quote from an academy instructor to recruits in Joseph Wambaugh's popular book *The New Centurions* should help drive this point home:

> *Maybe your man is going to decide you aren't going to handcuff him. Or maybe he'll even fight back. What I'm trying to do is tell you that these fights out there in the streets are just endurance contests. The guy who can endure usually wins.*

This is not TV aerobics chatter; it's real life on the streets and a real fight staring you in the face. As a training officer in the Philadelphia Police Department put it, "If you're not ready to lay your hands on someone and roll around in the gutter to get the guy under control, then you might as well just quit now and get a job selling shoes."

Like it or not, this is a violent job. You can ride round for seven hours and fifty-nine minutes without breaking a sweat. But if you aren't ready for that one solid minute of rolling-in-the-streets fighting, then you're no good to yourself, your partner, or your department. We don't all need to be built like Arnold Schwarzenegger or be able to run like Carl Lewis—most of us don't have the time or capability to achieve those fitness levels—but to survive and win in this job, you need to be in shape.

If that means taking up weight lifting, jogging, basketball, racquetball, or tennis, then so be it. Choose something that will make your body and your heart strong and stay with it. Too many cops die from stress-related diseases every year. It's not just the physical challenges on the street but the stress of the unknown that rides around in the car all day and night with you. Exercise will help you to relieve that stress. We've all heard stories about fat old cops dying of heart attacks while running after burglars. But you don't have to be old or fat to have a heart attack. Your body needs to be ready for the worst scenario your shift may offer.

Lastly, there is a certain phenomenon in exercise circles known as the "high." When everything is working right and you're operating like a well-oiled machine, you'll feel this natural energy lift. Runners get it near the end of a good run, and weight lifters refer to it as "the pump." Whatever you call it, the whole sensation is good for you, and you should strive for it.

The mental aspects of the high and the pump also carry over to your job as a police officer. When you feel good, you look good and vice versa. When you're in good shape, you know it, and the crooks know it, too. They watch us more than we watch them, so it pays to give the enemy something to think about.

Criminals and street people often think like animals. They evaluate their foes prior to any confrontation. If they think there is the distinct possibility of losing, they'll probably back down. Police officers who are fit and trim exude a sense of self-confidence that even the lowest street lizard can't ignore.

Can you afford not to be in the best shape of your life right now? The life you save *will be* your own. Being in good physical and mental condition should be a major part of your survival plan. One last note: the convicts from certain state prisons give a new parolee a T-shirt to remind him of his priorities in life. It reads:

> "BURN THEIR HOUSES,
> RAPE THEIR WIVES,
> EAT THEIR BABIES."

They are talking about us. They're ready to do battle. Are you?

Eyes in the Back of Your Head: Attack during Traffic Stops

Traffic-stop safety is a frequent topic of police magazine columns. Many officers have written excellent articles whose sole purpose is to remind you to be careful during a car stop.

Some confidential information concerning the training and tactics of known terrorist organization members makes the subject of traffic-stop safety even more critical.

Without revealing too much classified information, it's safe to say that if you've read any bulletins concerning these groups in years past, you can tell these people are not fooling around. The gist of the story coming from several criminal intelligence units around the country is that a certain group of paramilitary/terrorist thugs have established elaborate plans for murdering police officers during traffic-stop encounters. This information should make you reconsider your safety habits during every single traffic stop you make from now on. It's that serious.

Many organized terrorist groups rely on the expertise of former and current military (and police) personnel to advise them on such things as weapons, explosives, and diversionary tactics. Unfortunately, few police officers (except for SWAT members) have had recent training in these areas, even if they do have extensive military backgrounds. The advantage in weaponry, firepower, and assault tactics is clearly on the side of the terrorists. That's why we have to use what we have plenty of: intelligence, street safety awareness, and the desire to survive any dangerous encounter.

The murderous tactics of these people show us they have clear-cut plans for cop killing during any possible contact with the police. As an example, these people like to finance their operations with armored car or bank robberies. In a robbery situation involving the police, the lead car would contain the suspects, and the trailing car would be driven by so-called "normal" people, usually a man and a woman, neatly dressed.

During any traffic stop of the first car, this "average-looking" pair in the rear car becomes cop killers. This should reiterate that you cannot judge people solely by their appearance. Men and women in nice clothing will kill you just as fast as any scruffy-looking dirtbag.

My feeling is that during any kind of traffic stop, another car that isn't a police vehicle should have no reason to pull up behind my parked unit. If I see a suspicious car come up behind mine during a stop, I'm going to take any action I need to protect myself, even if that means dropping my ticket book, pulling my gun, and calling for cover because I feel I'm being threatened.

The unfortunate part of this scenario is that there is no one "right" way to react. If you have hostile suspects in front of your car and another pair in back, you don't have many alternatives for cover, unless you're near a concrete wall or something similar.

While this rock-and-a-hard-place scenario is difficult at best, you can try several alternatives. One technique used successfully in Vietnam during ambush assaults is to turn, face your opponents, and return immediate fire. In most ambush cases, the attacker expects you to be confused, frightened, and preoccupied with looking for a place to hide. The idea is to turn as soon as you see the hostile threat from the rear car, draw your weapon, and fire multiple rounds downrange at them. These people expect you to look for cover before you begin to shoot, so you can take advantage of this perception of you.

If you can pump a number of rounds at the rear suspects, you may take them by surprise. The second key to this attack technique is to move toward the suspects as you fire. Remember that the suspects in the first car are still a threat to you. If you can eliminate the rear suspects by firing and moving in their direction, you may be able to position yourself behind their car so you can deal with the front group. This way, you put the second group's car and your patrol car between you and the first set of suspects.

I'll admit these ideas seem contrary to your training (i.e., cover and concealment, target acquisition, etc.,) and even counterinstinctive, but we're talking about a life-and-death situation where there is no sure way to win.

Whatever you choose to do, the point is to not just stand there with your head buried in your ticket book and let someone sneak up and kill you. If you feel you may be threatened by someone coming up on foot or in a car, drop what you're doing and move, with gun in hand if necessary.

A story from a veteran officer explains the wisdom of this tactic. In the early 1980s, a cop killer in the San Francisco area used a similar tactic to shoot several officers. He would wait until he saw an officer writing a ticket before he approached. Witnesses reported that he usually had a map or what looked like a fix-it ticket in his hand. He would come up near the officer and say, "Oh, I can see you're busy. I'll just wait over here."

The officer would usually nod his head as the suspect stepped way and then continue to write his ticket, not bothering to give the suspect any more attention. Just some guy wanting directions or a cite signed off, right? Wrong! As soon as the officer's guard was down, the suspect would shoot him in the back.

Just because someone looks harmless doesn't mean you shouldn't treat him or her like any other street person until you know otherwise. If this person wants something from you, take care of it and send him along. Put the person between you and the car you've stopped so you can watch both of them. Turning your back on a person in the street or a car you've just stopped is never a good idea, whether you're alone or with a partner.

The bottom line is that if you don't know what's going on, don't wait to find out. Wouldn't you rather write an entire carton of reports explaining to a supervisor why someone thinks you overreacted than have homicide detectives explain to your family how you failed to move when faced with multiple armed suspects and multiple vehicles?

Nobody was born with eyes in the back of his or her head, but if you want to survive in this job, you need to develop the power to see behind you and know what to do during any kind of contact. After you've made a stop, continue to pay attention to your surroundings, not just to the stopped car or the citation in your hand. Pay attention all around you, on both sides, and even above. If you see this car-stop murder scenario developing, and this is becoming increasingly more likely in the future, you should already know what to do and where to go.

A Fast Buckle-Up: Driver Movement during Stops

Mandatory seat belt laws across the nation have added a new dimension of danger for officers making traffic stops. Since no one really wants a ticket for this violation, I'm sure you're seeing more and more people fumbling with their belts when you approach the car. These furtive movements can send off warning signals that could easily be misinterpreted by an approaching officer.

An internal memo given to Los Angeles Police Department (LAPD) officers on the subject of the quick buckle-up hit home: "Field officers are noting reactions by motorists which are consistent with threats to officer safety." Spokesmen from other law enforcement agencies say their officers are seeing the same type of driver behavior over and over when they make traffic stops.

The LAPD made a training film about the potential problems relating to quick seat-belt buckling. The purpose of the film is to guard against overreaction by approaching officers. However, one member of the LAPD top brass has to be credited with one of the more puzzling statements about the subject of evasiveness on the part of traffic violators and its effect on officer safety. He said, "We can't be pulling our guns over every furtive movement."

My question is "Why not?" That kind of logic could prove fatal. I see no reason to assume that just because you can't see someone's hands as you walk up to the car, that he or she is in the process of buckling up. The person could be hiding dope, putting a beer can under the seat, reaching for a knife, or feeling around the armrest for a gun. You know what happens when you "assume" anything in police work.

I also realize that the LAPD and other police agencies may have had some citizen complaints over officers scaring "innocent" citizens who were merely trying to save themselves a few citation dollars. The whole issue is indeed a gray area.

But, since it's your life and your peace of mind, wouldn't you risk a complaint and consider reaching for your weapon if someone dropped his or her hands quickly out of sight as you approached the car?

I'm not saying every traffic stop where you believe the fast buckle-up is happening should cause you to draw your gun. Yet we all know which stops "feel right" and which ones don't. If the traffic violator makes a movement you feel threatens your safety, then you shouldn't hesitate to take any appropriate action to control the situation.

Why not at least have your hand on your gun, or have it partway out of the holster if you see these furtive movements, which may or may not be valid? The time to decide what to do is before things go down the tubes. If the stop goes sour, then at least you have your hand on the right piece of police equipment for the job. As the old adage goes, "The fastest drawn gun is the one that's already in your hand."

Sometimes when you approach you can see the shoulder harness moving, and that should tell you the fast buckle-up is in progress. But what about older cars—like Mustangs, Volkswagen Bugs, or pick-up trucks—that have no shoulder harnesses?

Clearly, it's not safe or smart to take anything for granted. A simple way to prevent these tricky misunderstandings would be to use your PA or a loud voice command to warn the driver to keep his or her hands in plain sight as you approach.

I'll gladly risk a complaint from a driver who thought I "overreacted" because I had my hand near my gun or my gun even out of the holster entirely. Let's look at it this way: I don't know what the traffic violator does for a living, where he has just come from, or what he has just done. On the other hand, he knows everything about me—what I do and what I'm there for. Don't assume anything.

We all know that crooks like to keep their knives, sawed-off shotguns, ice picks, and other nasty devices in the hollowed-out door panels of their junky old cars. Unfortunately, this is near an area where many seat belts lie when the driver doesn't use them.

Don't point your weapon at anybody unless it's absolutely necessary. With your gun at your side and behind your hip, you can quickly determine the nature of the contact. Then you can unobtrusively reholster your weapon and continue with the stop.

Each stop and contact is different. (Notice I didn't say, "routine.") The traffic conditions, the weather, the lighting, the location, and the preestablished risk level all play an important part in every stop. If you can't see someone's hands, then that person should get your full attention. If that means you have to pull your gun in one form or another, then so be it. If the only thing the driver is reaching for is a seat belt, then you may be safe. But if his or her hands are reaching for a weapon, you'll be in a good position to deal with the threat.

Old habits die hard, especially when it comes to driving. While traffic experts say we are certainly seeing success with mandatory seat-belt laws, it will take some time—and some consistent enforcement—to remind everyone to use their belts. Until we get 100-percent compliance (read that as never), you can expect to see the fast buckle-up during some traffic stops. Watch those hands!

Field Interview and Radio Call Basics

Here's a quick overview of what you know you should already be doing out there. No surprises, just some sound advice for the street officer. Are you deviating from these basic safety tactics or not? Ask yourself these questions:

- How often do I drive by potential robbery locations on my beat? Have I made a tactical action plan for them? Can I practice "invisible deployment" to get near them without being seen? No practice means I'm never ready. Contingency plans are not a game.
- Do I keep up my guard on alarms—silent, false, or otherwise? Do I treat all silent alarm calls as if they were real crimes in progress?
- If I need my gun or baton, have I practiced with it lately? Practiced reloading in the dark? Practiced reloading with either hand?
- Do I keep in mind that the majority of shootings during traffic stops happen during the early stages of the stop? Do I keep my eyes on the suspect before approaching? Do I watch the traffic violator's hands at all times? Do I check traffic before I get out of my car on stops? Consider that nearly 50 percent of all officers

killed on car stops were hit by passing cars.

- Do I ever put my back to the violator's car? Do I look up during ticket writing? Do I maintain a good field-interview stance at all times?
- Do I use extra caution during drunk-driving stops? Am I always aware of the increased likelihood of assault or escape because the drunk driver knows there is a good possibility he or she will go to jail?
- Do I use caution when people come toward me as I sit in the patrol car? Do I talk to people from the car, or do I get out and come to them?
- Do I use the same caution when arresting females as I do with males? Do I use approved pat-down techniques for females? Do I search all females I arrest— not just their purses?
- Do I tell the suspect what he or she is being arrested for to prevent a "self-defense" assault claim later in court?
- Do I watch the suspect's hands and body position as I approach? Do I do a visual pat-down? Do I stand out of arm's length of the suspect, using a bladed stance? Do I look up from the field-interview pad?
- When alone, do I keep suspects together so they won't circle around me?
- With another officer, do I practice the tactics of Contact & Cover?
- Am I paying attention to my attitude when dealing with the public? Do I get irritated at everybody, whether they deserve it or not?

This is all basic stuff, but it never hurts to get a little reminder now and then.

Fifty Officer Survival Tips

At the start of each new year, law-enforcement types like to say, usually after many glasses of highly spirited grog, "Yeah, this is really the year I'm gonna lose weight, start jogging, cut down on booze and junk food, and just be a healthier, stronger person, inside and out."

Right. The next morning, while the first hangovers of the New Year fight for recognition inside their throbbing heads, they realize that they just aren't up to a year's worth of pain and sacrifice. The infamous promises fall by the wayside.

To prevent this problem, I'm offering a choice from the following list of fifty New Year's officer survival resolutions. Pick the ones you like and stick to them. If others don't pertain to you, ignore them and go on about your life. Each of the resolutions has something to do with police work in some form or another. You may already be doing some of them. Others may sound too awful to even contemplate on an empty stomach, and still others might become part of your overall plan to lead a long, healthy, and safe life.

So with the element of choice in mind, you will plan to:

1. Break a sweat at least three times per week by lifting

something heavy, either weights or your body by doing freehand exercises like push-ups, pull-ups, and sit-ups.

2. Raise your heart rate at least three times per week with some kind of cardiovascular work, either running, cycling, swimming, or aerobics.

3. Take extra time to strengthen your back and stomach muscles. This will help keep you off the light duty and medically retired lists.

4. Eat more-balanced meals at home, including fewer fats, moderate proteins, and higher complex carbohydrates like pasta, rice, and fruit.

5. Eat better meals during meal breaks. Bring a lunch from home. Eat healthier sandwiches, fruits and salads, chicken, turkey, and fish instead of greasy eggs, bacon, sausage, pancakes, or hamburgers and fries.

6. Cut down on the amount of coffee, tea, and sodas you drink. Remember, one can of diet soda can have up to thirty-five milligrams of salt and a boatload of caffeine in it. Drink more water.

7. Give up high-calorie, tooth-rotting sweets. Eat fruit and fruit-sweetened foods instead. Try to avoid any foods with ingredients that end in "-ose," as in fructose, glucose, sucrose, lactose, etc.

8. Cut down on the booze and cigarettes. Enough said.

9. Drive more carefully, using a seat belt when necessary, especially during pursuits.

10. Check you car thoroughly before getting into it, especially the tires. Look for fresh dents, damage, missing parts, leaks, etc. Do this at the station and each time you come back from a lengthy radio call.

11. Practice at the range at least once per month, using your department's approved rounds to improve with each session.

12. Clean your firearm every month, which you'll need to do anyway because you'll be faithfully making those trips to the range.

13. Do some kind of defensive tactics work at least once

per month. Practice some handholds, hit a boxing bag with your fists and baton, spar with someone else, shadow box, or do any kind of activity that simulates "hands-on" arrest movements.

14. Attend all Advanced Officer Training (AOT) classes and sign up for at least one extra AOT class on narcotics, defensive tactics, etc., at least once per watch.

15. Go to an all-day officer survival seminar, watch some training videotapes, or read some new books on street safety.

16. Buy at least one complete new uniform per year with your uniform check.

17. Replace all your old or damaged equipment, including jackets, gloves, rain gear, handcuff cases and cuffs, Mace cans, speedloaders, holsters, helmets and face shields, whistles, ammo, and first-aid supplies.

18. Clean out your locker, especially those moldy towels.

19. Buy a good pair of sunglasses for first and second watch and a fan and heater for comfy sleeping at home after summer and winter graveyards.

20. Buy a new *Penal Code* and highlight the changes.

21. Get a new *Vehicle Code* and highlight the changes, using your cite book cheat sheet.

22. Get a new map book and highlight your beats and boundaries.

23. Buy a new battery pack for your Streamlight.

24. Buy a good cassette tape or book of Spanish (or the predominant minority language in your area) phrases for cops and practice enough to be able to actually use them in the field.

25. Practice deep relaxation and stress control using a self-hypnosis tape at least twice a week for twenty minutes.

26. Buy yourself a new set of clothes for court appearances.

27. Organize your ticket book and report box, throwing out the outdated forms and replacing them with current ones.

28. Get a new box of rubber gloves and some fresh hand cleaner.

29. Collect and read "Be on the Lookout" (BOL) sheets provided by your detectives and teletype. Keep them in a notebook for use as probable cause in the street.

30. Read all the legal update and department policy material when it comes out.

31. Organize and update your policies and procedures manual.

32. Review your radio procedures and get rid of any lazy or long-winded habits.

33. Review your response to low-risk calls, such as burglary or auto-theft reports. Park tactically, bring all of your equipment, and keep your gun hand free.

34. Review your domestic-violence call responses. Approach carefully, watch for weapons, and separate the parties in a way that offers maximum safety for you and your partner.

35. Review your "hot call" responses. Park, approach, and search with caution during alarm ringers. During robbery calls, park tactically and use the proper procedures to locate and arrest any suspects.

36. Since misdemeanor arrests seem to waste everyone's time, concentrate on putting more felony crooks into jail.

37. Take more beat responsibility. Put your problem children in jail and make summer or winter projects out of these potential problem children on your beat.

38. Review your pat-down and searching procedures. Remember to search in quadrants, watching for sharp objects in pockets, cuffs, and hats. and gloves

39. Review your report-writing procedures. Remember to fill in all the appropriate boxes and try to put out a little extra effort to make it easier for the prosecutors and detectives who have to read your work.

40. Improve your accident reports by making careful and complete diagrams—including lane measurements. Get all of the appropriate witness, insurance, and vehicle damage information before sending the parties on their way.

41. Take steps to improve your grammar, spelling, punc-

tuation, and word choice with your reports. Strive to be brief, clear, and complete with every report you sign your name to.

42. Review your safety habits concerning your vehicle and pedestrian stop procedures.

43. Review your firearms-handling techniques, especially with shotguns.

44. Review all of the elements of Contact & Cover, including the hand signals and the roles and responsibilities of each officer.

45. Buy something that's just for you. Maybe a new gun, a bicycle, something for your house or car, or maybe just a new "toy."

46. Take at least one goof-off day per watch to rest and restore your energy and enthusiasm for the job.

47. Spend more time with your spouse and kids if you have them or with your main squeeze if you don't.

48. Be more tolerant of citizens and even dirtbags. Everybody has a side to tell. Take some patience pills before you jump in at disturbances, traffic citations, and car-accident calls.

49. Be more tolerant of your supervisors and fellow officers, especially rookies and trainees who are still trying to grasp the various aspects of this job.

50. Finally, spend some time before each shift thinking about the important people in your life—family, spouse, children, and friends. These people care about you, and you owe it to them and yourself to do whatever you need to do to be safe and secure.

Freeway Stops

Like it or not, freeway stops are a part of this job. For all the inherent dangers and inconveniences, we have to take control of any situation on the freeway for our own safety and the safety of the vehicle we pull up behind. We have all heard stories about officers who were killed while directing traffic, writing tickets, or laying flare patterns at an accident site on the freeway.

Whether you're nabbing a flagrant speeder or providing help to a stranded motorist, you must follow certain life-saving rules on the freeway.

Since most state traffic officers (or troopers) spend the majority of their time on freeways, they know how to make safe and effective freeway stops. Most of these officers write an average of ten to thirty tickets per shift, five days a week, all year long. That adds up to a lot of freeway stops.

A veteran trooper offers this series of safety tips for police officers who have to make freeway stops during the day or at night. Some of the tips you may already know and practice most of the time. Some of the tips relate specifically to freeway stops and are extremely important.

Safe Locations for Stops

Know the freeways leading to and from your beat. Become familiar with the road conditions, shoulder areas, number of lanes, and potential hazards driving to and from the station, jail, or your patrol area. The more you know about the "lay of the land," the better chance you'll have to pick a safe location to make a freeway stop.

Just as you try to choose a well-lit, wide-shouldered area to make a traffic stop in the city, you need to meet the same considerations before you make a freeway stop. Try to plan your stop so you have a wide right shoulder area in the daytime and a well-lighted place at night.

Never make a stop in what is called the "gore point"— the V-shaped area dividing the freeway off-ramp exit and the rest of the road. This is an extremely hazardous place to stop, and if you or the violator is hit by a car, you could be found at fault.

Obviously, if you come upon a stalled car, you don't have much choice about the safety of the location. However, if you feel it's too dangerous, don't hesitate to push the car out to a clear area. Your safety is the primary factor.

As soon as you have picked your stop area, pull to a safe distance behind the violator and activate your emergency lights. Be very careful of any irrational maneuvers by either the car you want to stop or other cars around you.

Remember that many people get "black-and-white fever" when they see a police car in action. As soon as you have activated your overheads, put on your right blinker as a signal to the violator to pull to the right side of the freeway. This is a critical point: never make a stop on the left side of the road unless there is no other safe choice. If the driver stops on the shoulder next to the fast lane, use your PA to tell him or her you will follow his or her car to the right side of the road as soon as it is safe.

Be careful of changing road conditions. Construction trucks frequently drop gravel or sand on either side of the highway. Watch for these hazards or you could risk a rear-end accident if the violator stops quickly.

After you stop, turn off your overhead lights and leave your turn signal and your rear amber light on. Park your car in an off-set position at least ten feet away from the violator's car. Before you get out of your car, turn your wheels all the way to the left. Making this sharp angle for your front wheels is critical to your safety. If your car were to get hit from behind, the impact would send it to the left and out into traffic, instead of directly into the car you stopped.

I cannot overemphasize the importance of this last step. Get into this habit right now so it will become second-nature for you. Develop this safety practice on all of your stops, on the freeway or in the city.

Approaching a Stopped Vehicle

Try to exit your car as quickly and safely as possible, watching the violator at all times. As you approach the car, cross over and walk to the right side. When you get near the car, press down on the trunk lid as you pass to make sure no one is hiding in there, and watch the driver's movements.

Look into the back and passenger seats and talk to the driver through the window on the right side of the car. For ultimate safety, you may want to face your car as you talk to the driver. This way you can see the driver, his car, your car, and the passing traffic.

Tell the driver to stay in the car, but if he or she comes out, get them over to the passenger side of the car immediately. For more safety, and depending on how you feel about the contact, you can take the driver back to the passenger side of your car to talk. If the driver has one or more passengers, you may want to take him or her out for your own safety.

If you walk back with the driver, have him or her stand between you and the stopped car. This way you can watch the driver and the passengers.

If the driver stays in the car after the contact, walk back to your passenger door or rear of the car and stand behind it to write the citation. Look up occasionally to watch the movement of the driver. Reapproach the car on the right side and have the driver sign the citation through the passenger window.

It is also your responsibility to make sure the driver doesn't get into an accident once he or she leaves the shoulder. Remember to warn the driver to pull out only when it's safe to do so.

Night stops offer more hazards because of reduced visibility, so you need to be especially careful. Once you decide to stop a car, it's up to you to get the driver over to the right side of the road as safely as possible. Be careful not to blind the driver with your hand spot as you pull over.

As with daytime stops: before you get out, remember to cock your wheels to the left, turn off your overheads to the amber light, put on your high beams, and aim your spot into the driver's mirror.

As soon as you get out of your car to approach, turn on your flashlight beam, hold it at the side of your leg with the beam shining behind you, and quickly shake it back and forth, aiming it toward approaching traffic. Before you approach, use the movement of this light as a signal to passing cars that you're out of your vehicle. When you get near the violator's car, you can aim it into the window. Use your light to check the back and passenger sides of the car as you watch the driver. Follow the other steps as outlined for daytime stops.

Remember, your safety depends on how well the oncoming traffic can see you. Stay out of the lanes as much as you can, use your car for a shield, and pay attention to the traffic around you.

Laying Flares at Accident Sites

Laying flare patterns on the freeway presents another

problem. You may be forced to lay dozens of flares at a large accident until other officers and fire and ambulance people can respond.

Remember, given freeway speeds, you must lay the flares well ahead of the accident so other vehicles have time to see the obstruction and make the necessary changes in their driving. One other tip: if you have to direct traffic at an accident scene, try to put at least three or four flares directly in front of you. The combination will put out more light and help you stand out to passing cars.

▼　▼　▼　▼　▼

Freeway stops are not easy, and many officers don't look forward to exposing themselves to the dangers. Yet, with stranded motorists and the increasing number of speeders and reckless drivers on our freeways, we have to know how to make these stops safely and effectively.

Handling Narcotics: Watch What You Touch!

Drugs are covering this nation from one coast to the other. From the large, urban cities to the small, rural town, the buzzword from both the politician and the police officer is drugs.

Since the problem is a real one, the street officer faces a number of hazards during a typical narcotics arrest. The threat from the suspect or suspects is constant, but a narcotics arrest also presents other dangers, namely, from the contraband itself.

Handling narcotics calls for special precautions. In the heat and danger of the arrest, it's easy to forget about the poisonous substances in your hands or in the air you breathe. Some of this may sound like basic stuff, but if you don't work in a particularly high-narcotics area, it can serve as a good review of your arrest procedures.

Let's look at a few common narcotics arrest scenarios:

- You stop a suspect just after he has purchased a small quantity of heroin. It's in a syringe and ready to go into his arm. When you find him, the needle is sticking out of his front shirt pocket, point out. What do you do?
- You stop several gang members and immediately

smell the strong odor of ether. One of the suspects has a small brown bottle in his jacket pocket. Another suspect has several brown cigarettes in his pants pocket. What do you do?

• You make a car stop carrying several teenagers. You smell marijuana, and you see two burning joints in the ashtray, along with several other half-burned ones. What do you do?

The answer in each case is to first isolate, subdue, and confine the suspect or suspects. You need to first protect yourself and your partner from attack and, secondly, to protect the evidence from destruction, spoilage, or exposure.

Get the suspect into handcuffs as soon as possible, then deal with the evidence. The last thing you want is to get into a wrestling match with a person armed with a needle or a vial of PCP.

Today's police officer is equipped with many tools, including a duty weapon, handcuffs, Mace, baton, and—most importantly in the 1990s—a pair of latex rubber gloves. If you work with the public, you need to carry several pairs of gloves.

Let's go back to our examples: In the first case, the needle sticking out of the shirt pocket presents several distinct dangers, including the threat of exposure to whatever drug is in the syringe, hepatitis, or even the AIDS virus. You need to get the suspect cuffed and secured so he can't twist around as you carefully remove the needle. If at all possible, make sure you have your gloves on. Try to remove the needle by grasping the body of the syringe, not the needle itself. Carry it by the body and keep the point away from you and other officers at all times.

Transportation, storage, and impounding of needles is another concern. One method involves placing all pointed objects into the glove compartment of your patrol car. Use some fingerprinting tape to attach the needle to a small piece of cardboard. This way, you can safely transport the needle and don't have to worry about losing it or its getting stuck.

At the very least, wrap some tape around the needle portion of the syringe. These methods also help to protect the property and lab personnel from exposure. Remember to write "NEEDLE" across the impound envelope.

Let's go back to the second arrest scenario. The strong smell of ether should immediately alert you that you're dealing with PCP suspects. Since the drug is commonly transported in dark colored bottles, you can assume the first suspect is carrying liquid PCP. And since brown cigarettes known as "Shermans" or "Sherms" are commonly dipped in liquid PCP, you can assume your second suspect is also carrying it.

The rule of thumb is the same. Isolate the suspects, cuff them quickly, and wear your rubber gloves prior to touching the evidence. Remove the bottle carefully and make sure it is tightly capped. Do not smell it or allow any of the substance to spill on your skin or clothing. PCP can be absorbed through the skin. Use the same technique to remove the PCP-laced cigarettes. Be careful not to smell them or allow them to touch your exposed skin.

Transporting PCP requires extra precautions. If the drug spills and exposes you to the fumes or liquid, the results could be horrifying. One LAPD officer, splashed with PCP during a drug raid, suffered hallucinations, headaches, and other disabilities so severe he had to retire from the department and still suffers from the effects of the exposure.

Impounding PCP calls for other safety precautions. Since the drug is so toxic, you must seal it in an airtight container, such as a heat-sealed bag. Refer to your department's own guidelines for further help.

Remember also to wear your gloves when you deal with PCP suspects who may not necessarily be in possession of the drug. Their clothes, skin, car seats, etc., may have been exposed to the drug. You could receive a nasty "contact high" if you're not careful.

Let's look at the third narcotics arrest scenario. Unfortunately, those teenagers may not be smoking a few "harmless" joints. They could be laced with PCP, crack, or an opiate. You must treat all narcotics as if they were potentially poisonous.

Isolate and arrest the suspects, even if you only plan to cite and release them. With the suspects safely out of your way, you can put on your rubber gloves, extinguish and remove the joints, and secure them for impounding later.

One additional rule for impounding marijuana: never touch the contraband with ungloved hands. Some officers use good safety habits while in the field, only to handle the dope carelessly while weighing or bagging it.

Remember to treat every narcotic substance as if it were laced with a poison. Never smell, touch, or taste any suspected narcotic substance. It could be marijuana, a PCP-laced cigarette, black-tar heroin, or Drano-filled amphetamine capsules. Wear your gloves. They can provide you with cheap life insurance. Search carefully, remove the narcotics in a safe manner, transport the drugs to the station, and use proper procedures to impound these scourges of today's society.

High Risk In Means High Risk Out

It's a bright sunny day, and you're driving around aimlessly on your beat. A car catches your eye as it rolls through a stop sign. You make a quick U-turn and pull up behind the car and hit your emergency lights. The driver doesn't pull over immediately and takes you on a brief thirty-five-miles-per-hour tour of the neighborhood. Finally, after some horn-honking, finger-pointing, and siren-yelping, he yields to the right side of the road.

You get out and approach his car. A passenger pops up from the back seat with a wild look on his face. He turns and says something to the driver, who immediately floors the gas pedal and speeds away, leaving you halfway between his car and yours. You hotfoot it back to your unit and begin the chase again.

After advising radio of your location and direction, you get some cover units to assist with the stop. The driver eventually yields on a residential street, with three cop cars now behind him. So what happens after you and the other officers set your cars in park? Chaos takes over, and common sense flies out the window.

Cops come from all directions and rush up to the suspect vehicle, guns drawn, commands at the ready. Some officers run up to the driver's side and some to the passenger side, all with the intent of jerking said occupants through the wing windows. After much laying on of hands, the result is usually two suspects in custody and high blood-pressure rates all around.

Okay, how about this scenario: you and your partner are sitting in a convenience-store parking lot reminiscing about the old days when you hear a motorcycle pursuit come out over the air. The suspect is a few miles away from your present location, so you decide to start up the car and pick a likely stakeout spot. En route to that location, you hear the primary pursuit units say they have lost the suspect in your vicinity. Suddenly, the motorcycle zooms by you in a blur of metal and leather.

You jump on his tail and finally catch him in a cul-de-sac. You slam the car into park, and you and your partner do what? You sprint toward this biker and heave him onto the pavement, motorcycle and all.

Okay, last scenario: Working alone, you stop a suspected drunk driver. When you approach the car, the driver is belligerent and uncooperative. You get him out of the car, and he challenges you to a fight. After forty-five seconds of pain compliance and wrist twists, he gives up and you get the bracelets on him. All the way down to jail he is abusive and hostile. In line at jail, he threatens your family. Once inside, what do you do? You take his cuffs off and tell him to put his hands on the wall until the intake deputy is ready for him.

What's the common factor in each of these scenarios? They all involve motor vehicles? Sort of. They all involve suspected dirtbags? Not completely. They all happened outside? Not necessarily.

The common theme in each of these events is the *risk*. Each of these scenarios involves an element of risk to your health and safety. Drivers who flee after you get out of your car, motorcyclists who take officers all over the city, and hostile drunks are all high-risk candidates. They should be treated as such at all times, from the moment your actual contact begins until they're on the other side of the jail door and you're heading for your car.

Proper High-Risk Procedures

Let's review the scenarios again to see the mistakes. In the first situation, you know after the driver flees that this is not a normal car stop. The driver and his passenger have exhibited high-risk behavior. What might happen if you leap from your car and run up to their vehicle? You could get shot. In your haste to "make the pinch" you can stray into the suspect's ambush range. For this type of pursuit, you must initiate high-risk vehicle stop techniques. Get out of your car and assume the high-risk stop position: "Driver! Police! Get your hands up!"

Your cover units should assume their respective high-risk vehicle stop roles and cover you until all suspects are cleared from the car. To do it any other way is to let your guard down and risk being shot. Follow the axiom: "High risk going in means high risk coming out."

In the second scenario, the motorcycle rider has definitely shown his high-risk tendencies. To approach him on foot while he straddles the bike is to risk being shot, stabbed, or otherwise injured by the suspect or his motorcycle.

Again, initiate high-risk vehicle stop procedures: "Driver! Police! Hands up!" Have the suspect kill his engine, raise his hands, put the kickstand down on the bike, and step off of it. You can then use felony kneeling techniques to take him into custody. Why risk injury by wrestling with the suspect and his motorcycle? High risk in, high risk out.

Lastly, what about the obnoxious drunk driver? Didn't he show his high-risk behavior by refusing to cooperate and even fighting with you? What might happen when you take his cuffs off and order him to put his hands on the jail door?

If he really doesn't care about his well-being, you could find yourself fighting for your life before the deputies can help you. Tell the deputies if your suspect is a fighter. Keep him in handcuffs until they can control him. High risk in, high risk out.

In the heat of the moment, we all want to do the right thing—grab the crook and make the arrest as quickly as possible. Remember that time is on your side. You don't have to perform any heroics that might get you hurt or killed. Use the high-risk techniques you've been taught. Just because a suspect "gives up" and lets you begin to cuff him doesn't mean he won't try to hurt you later.

It's like the old story about the man who finds the injured snake in the woods. He takes the snake home and nurses it back to health. Later, as he is releasing the snake back into the forest, it coils up and bites him on the arm. "Why did you do that?" said the man, rubbing his arm and wincing. "I nursed you back to health!"

"Yes, that's true" said the snake, "but you knew I was a snake when you took me home."

High-risk in; high-risk out.

The Hollywood Ten: TV Cops' Tactical Errors

Planted on the sofa, remote control at the ready, you're bound to see a wide variety of strange, dull, or fascinating fare coming from the glowing vacuum tube we call television. From sports to soaps and from Oprah to Letterman, you can cover the broad spectrum loosely known as "entertainment."

No matter how much TV changes, it always stays the same. There are innumerable commercials, tedious news "teasers," and, above all, cop shows. From "Car 54, Where Are You?" and Broderick Crawford in "Highway Patrol," we've shot it out with the TV cops of "Police Story" (my favorite), and on into the doldrums of the night with "Police Woman," "McCloud," "Starsky and Hutch," "T.J. Hooker," "S.W.A.T.," "Hunter," "Baretta," "Hill Street Blues," and the forever-fashionable MTV cops on "Miami Vice."

While watching some "lone-wolf detective" cop show one night, I realized that over the twenty-plus years I've viewed cop shows and movies, I've also seen the same tactical errors over and over again. You know the kind I mean. You say to yourself, or to any other noncop in the room, "Geez, why did he do that? I could write better shows than this. Why don't they ask me to be a technical advisor for this stuff? No cops would ever be that stupid in real life."

Or would they? As much as we like to criticize the cookie-cutter plots and the "shots fired, back to work in ten minutes" mentality, the tactical errors from Hollywood often mirror our own mistakes. I'm not saying we screw up like those pretend cops on TV, but some of their errors may look more familiar than we want to admit.

Let's look at what I call "The Hollywood Ten." This list represents the major tactical flaws you might see during an average prime-time cop show. See which ones you recognize and, more importantly, which ones you may unwittingly commit yourself.

1. *Gun pointed straight up while moving.* During a tactical seminar I attended, Illinois SWAT expert Andrew J. Casavant referred to this as "The Sabrina" position, made famous by one of the female characters on that fine police show "Charlie's Angels." If your gun needs to be out of your holster, keep it horizontal and on target. It takes too much time to pull it level, find your target, and fire.

2. *Gun too far away from body during building search.* This is a classic. We always see TV cops hugging the wall with their gun arm exposed and extended. What usually happens when they cross a doorway? The crooks chop at their wrist, and the struggle is on. If your gun is drawn, keep it close to your body, using your elbows to brace against your ribs. Stay away from the wall and use shadows or the well-known "pizza-cutting" angle of approach for rooms.

3. *Standing too close to suspect.* This is another classic, also known as the "In Your Face" interrogation technique. What usually happens when you violate your suspect's "space"? A fight ensues, with you on the ground and him screaming curses in your ear. Stay back; give yourself some room.

Adjust to a shift in your suspect's position by moving tactically to the side. Maintain a minimum reaching distance, but get out of the suspect's face.

4. *Finger-pointing.* Think about how much you hate it when someone does this to you. Waving your digit at a crook just encourages a smart remark, a fistfight, or a complaint.

5. *Barehanded fistfights.* God loves police officers. Why else did He give us so many "impact instruments" to use instead of our brittle hand bones? Use your stick, Mace, bodyweight, or, best yet, the assistance of another officer. You get no sympathy if you break your hand on some hood's bony forehead. Think about a large and heavy cast over your knuckles before you decide to swing that big roundhouse.

6. *Bad or no cover during shootout.* Clint Eastwood as "Dirty Harry" epitomizes this one. Remember how he could walk calmly down the street as the crooks were shooting a barrage of rounds at him? Bullets whizzed by his head with hardly a passing glance. TV and movie cops are bulletproof. We know that. Where else do you see an entire house, car, building, etc., get shot up by machine-gun rounds with nary a scratch on our hero? We are not so fortunate or lucky. Practice firing, unloading, and loading behind cover during your next session at the range.

7. *Losing sight of the suspect during foot pursuit.* Very dangerous. Remember how you've been taught. It's always better to gather the troops and return for a thorough search than to risk an ambush. We've seen the deadly effects of foot chases on many police departments.

8. *Not watching behind you for other suspects.* This is known in Hollywood as the "Final Insult." Our hero is just getting ready to save the day when—out of nowhere—

another crook puts a gun in his ear and takes him hostage. Think about all our gangbangers cruising in their "def rides." While you're on a traffic stop with one, his pals may come driving by in another vehicle. No cop likes the word "drive-by" used in any context. Watch your back while writing tickets, conducting field interviews, and making radio calls. Protect your partner and work as if you have eyes in the back of your head.

9. *No cover units.* Dumb, dumb, dumb. Hollywood cops get paid to say, "I'll handle this myself." We do not. Enough said.

10. *Nonexistent reports.* No list of Hollywood police errors would be complete without this one. It's a long-standing favorite of mine. Our hero saves the city after a seventy-five-car pileup, a 5,000-round shootout, and a fifteen-minute wrestling match with Godzilla's brother-in-law. Wiping the sweat from his sturdy brow, he heads home for a cold one. Hah! Good (real) cops write good (real) reports.

I may have left out a few of your favorites, but if nothing else, this list reminds you that TV cops aren't trying to be perfect, just entertaining. *You* don't have that luxury with your own life. You have to be perfect. So hey, let's be careful out there.

Ice

Methamphetamine

When you think of Hawaii, certain images come to mind. You probably see shady palm trees, beautiful sandy beaches, pineapples, macadamia nuts, rum-filled drinks, and curvy hula girls. You certainly don't think about drugs, especially one so powerful that it threatens to overtake rock cocaine as the drug of choice for today's users.

Sad to say that a new and deadly form of crystal methamphetamine has surfaced in Hawaii, and it's on the way to the mainland like—if you'll pardon the island imagery again—a tidal wave. It's called meth "ice" because it closely resembles rock salt or rock-candy crystals. It may look pretty, but it's dangerous and even fatal for a growing group of users.

Ice, also known as "crystals" or "batu" in Hawaii, gets its power from its purity. Whereas common street meth may have been "stepped on" or cut with other chemicals many times before it reaches the average doper, ice meth is 98- to 100-percent pure methamphetamine. To paraphrase Mark Twain, it's like the difference between a lightning bug and a lightning bolt.

According to officials from the Honolulu Police Narcotics Division, Hawaii is the primary U.S. source for ice because the drug comes from labs in Asia, especially Korea, Taiwan, and Singapore. Hawaiian narcs say they sent some ice samples to a lab for analysis, but the scientists had a difficult time retracing the process that puts it into the solid crystallized form. Drug Enforcement Administration (DEA) lab teams have also analyzed ice to determine how the drug is transformed into the large crystal form.

According to Honolulu Police, it's already reached epidemic proportions in Hawaii since its arrival in the early part of 1987. But don't think the island paradise holds the patent on ice, because it's also permeating mainland states such as California, Texas, Arizona, and Florida.

What makes ice meth so popular, and why is it such a problem for law enforcement? To answer these questions, we need to look at its history.

The synthetic drug methamphetamine was invented around 1919 by a Japanese chemist. Researchers found that the drug greatly accelerated and stimulated the central nervous system (CNS), which includes the brain, brain stem, and spinal cord. Widely used in 1930s, methamphetamine was prescribed by doctors for a variety of ailments, including depression, sleep disorders, and obesity. But the drug had some extreme side effects, as overuse led patients to strokes, heart attacks, pulmonary edema (retention of excess body fluids), prolonged comas, and even death. The drug was classified as a controlled substance soon after these findings became apparent.

So methamphetamine and its abuse is no stranger to the law enforcement community, from the federal level on down to the local police. We know meth is prevalent in this country because we deal with the paranoid, powder-snorting "tweakers" every day. Like cocaine, this drug shows no favorite boundary lines in terms of city or state geography; it's everywhere.

However, the key difference between standard run-of-the-mill "crank" and this new ice version is in its method of ingestion. Whereas powdered meth is snorted or injected, ice meth is smoked, and that difference accounts for the wild unpredictability of the drug and its abusers. Since the fumes from the drug are absorbed through the lungs, the intoxicating chemicals hit the brain much faster than if snorted.

Ice is smoked in glass pipes, which differ from crack pipes or dope "bongs" in their design. Crack pipes have two sections: one to hold the dope and the other to hold the liquid coolant. The sections are separated by a screen. As the drug burns, the user draws it up through the pipe, past the coolant, and into the mouth.

Ice pipes have only one section where the meth is heated. There are no coolers or screen on the devices. The pipes usually have a hole in the top of the bowl leading to the main chamber and a vent hole (called a "carb" on the streets) on the stem between the dope chamber and the mouthpiece. The user covers the vent hole with his or her finger and heats the ice until it turns into a gas. One clue to an ice user is the burn marks on the fingers used to cover the carb hole as the drug is smoked.

Clear ice is water-based and burns quickly, leaving a milky-white residue in the bowl. Yellow ice is oil-based and burns slowly, leaving a brown or black residue in the bowl. The drug is odorless when smoked, which is why the users like it; it doesn't give off a detectable smell like marijuana.

Dopers are switching to ice because it's much cheaper than cocaine and it offers a much longer high than coke or crack. The drug is sold in paper bindles or in heat-sealed plastic bags. The price for one hit—one-tenth of a gram—is about $50. It sells for around $250 to $400 per gram, which offers ten to twenty-five hits per user. An ounce may sell for as much as $7,000.

The high itself lasts up to fourteen hours, as opposed to only five minutes for a crack hit. What users don't realize is that ice is more physically addictive than heroin and the wildly depressive low points after the drug wears off can last for several days.

Ice users ride a physiological and emotional roller-coaster after using the drug. They are high four to fourteen hours, depending on the dosage. The drug enters the bloodstream rapidly, and large doses are excreted into the urine even up to seventy-two hours after use.

The intense purity of the drug and its effects on the CNS cause the body to literally "burn" itself up. Prolonged use will cause damage to the lungs, liver, and kidneys. Heavy psychological dependence can lead to a psychotic state, insomnia, anxiety, depression, fatigue, toxic psychosis, and delusions.

As with other drugs, heavy use means more needs to be used to feel the effects. Withdrawal may cause acute depression and fatigue, irritability, restlessness, tremors, talkativeness, insomnia, anxiety, delirium, panic, irregular heartbeat, dry mouth, nausea, vomiting, cramps, convulsions, coma, and even death.

For the street officer, spotting an ice user is fairly easy. The heavy ice smoker will exhibit most of the same symptoms as a meth snorter, including "blown" pupils, rapid heart and respiratory rate, and a hoarse voice from the burning in the throat. Users become paranoid and suspicious, lose sleep and weight, and generally feel like they're "going crazy."

But even with all these side effects, hypes are switching from heroin to ice because of its comparatively low price and because they think it's safer since no needles are involved. But unlike common meth heads, ice users have a frightening tendency to go through violent mood swings, not unlike users do when cycling through PCP.

Hawaiian ice is distributed by gang members in their twenties, which takes them out of the realm of the street punk and into the world of the criminal syndicate. As with the rock cocaine trade, the ice distribution network is filled with rivals fighting for control of Hawaii and points east. Gang leaders use ice to control their members physically, denying it or rewarding them with it for their work.

The drug is most commonly found on the island of

Oahu and in the city of Honolulu, but officers say it also appears on Kauai, Maui, and the big island of Hawaii. For now, the sale and use of meth ice is limited to Asia, Hawaii, and a few other U.S. states. But since our country seems filled with the type of doper who specializes in methamphetamine, don't be too surprised to see ice in wide use on your own streets soon. The subject has received wide play on local and national television programs. It's coming, and it's here to stay.

Interviewing Victims and Witnesses

Talking to crime victims and witnesses is a true art. Notice how some officers seem to get loads of information, while others only come away with the basics like name and address.

Dealing with the public on a daily basis demands total professionalism on your part. Keep in mind that while this may be the fifth burglary report of the day for you, it's probably the first one ever for the victim. And while you may have handled dozens of street robbery cases, your victim and witnesses are probably terrified and tongue-tied. Listen carefully and learn to ask the right questions at the right time. Here are some useful techniques to help improve your interviewing abilities:

- Conduct interviews in a quiet place if possible, especially out of earshot of the other witnesses to prevent one person from clouding everyone else's accounting of the facts.

- If possible, sit with the subject you're interviewing, making sure you sit at his or her eye level. Try to keep physical barriers—which might include a desk, the hood of a car, or even your sunglasses—from coming between you and the person with whom you're talking. These barriers can interfere with the communication process.

- Each time you interview someone in the field, that person is sizing you up, evaluating your attitude, trying to determine if you really care about his or her problem. Are you keeping your personal feelings out of the conversation? Are you aware of the impact that your own negative body language may have upon the conversation? This includes such negative signs as crossed arms, heavy sighing, rolling your eyes, etc.

- Establishing rapport and trust is the key to getting good information from people. One good trust-building technique is to wait for the person to tell you his or her version of the entire story before taking out your pen and pad.

- Toward the end of the interview, summarize the person's statement to you. This often helps a victim or witness to remember other facts. It's also a good way to wind up the interview in a polite fashion.

These techniques may sound simple, but some officers still violate many of them during daily field contacts. As an example, how many times have you taken a chronic domestic violence report and acted like the victim was wasting your time? Remember that most people rarely have any contact at all with the police. Talking to them in a professional, interested manner can make all the difference.

The Koga Method: Arrest and Control Techniques

Looking at Robert Koga, you get the immediate impression that the man is serious about his work. His face has a watchful, world-weary look about it. While not a particularly burly man, he seems to have intense inner strength. You can tell from the fluid way he moves that he has spent thousands of hours practicing and refining various martial-arts techniques.

As a cop in Los Angeles, Bob Koga worked various assignments in patrol, vice, homicide, narcotics, and intelligence, both as a patrol officer and an investigations supervisor. He has the gaze of someone who has seen it all. I suppose twenty-five years as a police officer in Los Angeles will do that to you.

His ten years' experience as an instructor at the LAPD Academy taught Koga that there was no uniform standard of training for recruits. Some instructors taught certain arrest and defensive techniques, while others favored completely different methods. There was no continuity of training, and Bob Koga could see his officers were getting injured and killed out on the streets because of it.

When he retired from LAPD, Bob established the Koga Institute of Arrest Control & Self-Defense. This program of

Practice at the range until you feel comfortable shooting, loading, and unloading your weapon with both hands. Can you operate your police tools with either hand? If so, great. If not, you know what to do.

A Long Three Minutes: Hostage-Suspect Confrontations

(This story is true; the names of all participants and the locations have been changed for privacy reasons.)

Death seemed to follow Officer Bob Ford that warm Saturday afternoon in Paradise Beach. He was working first watch and had spent most of the morning at a hospital with the family of a man who had died of a heart attack while jogging. Later that morning, only minutes after responding to a disturbance call, Bob had to shoot and kill Edward Wilson, a twenty-nine-year old male with a history of cocaine use. Wilson had taken his estranged wife hostage in his home and refused to put down his four-inch .38 revolver and give up. The time between when Bob and the other two officers arrived at the call and when the shots were fired was less than three minutes.

While Bob was leaving the hospital at approximately 11:45 A.M., a call came out, "Woman Being Held Against Her Will." Officer Sam Smith and his partner, Henry Harris, were assigned to the call along with another unit. Bob heard the second unit say he was responding from a distance, so he decided to cover as he was closer. He knew that with the noontime traffic that notoriously clogged up the area, he could make it to the scene sooner than the second unit.

• Some officers go so far as to put a P.O. Box on their checks. The theory behind this is to have all your department-related correspondence—motor vehicle registration and license information, police association material, police publications—come to a safe location away from your home.

• Think about taking different routes to and from your station. Stay in Condition Yellow at all times on the roads and in public.

• Be especially careful at fast-food restaurants, bars, banks, motels, parking lots, and liquor stores. Sit tactically in these places and keep a careful eye on the patrons. Three guys wearing overcoats in a summertime supermarket are nothing to ignore.

• Be especially careful how you drive and respond to bad drivers on the highways. Avoid a rolling "pissing contest" at all costs. Too many officers have been fired and/or sued for their behavior during these incidents.

• Watching other officers during FIs and traffic stops is always a good habit. Intervention, however, is another story. My feeling—and one voiced by most officers—is that I don't need you to help me unless I'm getting beat on or shot. Pulling up behind a cop on a traffic stop can frighten or confuse the officer and just make things worse by giving a real crook an opportunity to attack, escape, or destroy evidence. Watch officers during their FIs and traffic stops from a safe distance. You can intervene if necessary, but don't become part of the problem.

• Don't always be so quick to ID yourself as a cop. I remember hearing about an off-duty officer who tried to break up a bar fight with some good old-fashioned "command presence." He approached the two brawlers and reached into his back pocket for his badge. The smaller of the two fighters, who thought the officer was coming to help his opponent, smashed the officer in the face with a beer mug.

Telling the world you're a cop at a crisis situation may be necessary and practical to expedite help, but not always.

By identifying yourself as an officer, you immediately put the burden to "solve" any problem squarely on your shoulders. As a sage once said, "'Tis better to keep quiet and be thought a fool than to open your mouth and remove all doubts." Sometimes discretion is the better part of valor.

• Many supervisors have told me again and again, "Always remember your physical limitations during any potential off-duty confrontation. You probably don't have a vest, a baton, a radio, or a cover unit to protect you."

▼　▼　▼　▼　▼

Let's go back to our freeze-frame incident with the woman beater. Since we live in a highly imperfect world, there are no perfect solutions to this mess. There are other ways to handle it besides risking a punch-up or a shooting.

One way to solve this problem is to approach it tactically: when you see Johnny Dirtbag beating his woman, immediately tell your spouse to take your child back in the store and have someone call the police. Your spouse should already know what to tell the dispatcher if he or she makes the call or at least what to tell the store employee to say.

With help on the way, you can position yourself at a safe distance from the suspect and observe his actions. You'll want to memorize his complete physical description and that of any vehicle he may have nearby. You'll want to be ready to point him out to arriving units and to assist them if they ask.

Should you intervene with guns or fists in this situation? That's a hard choice, and one you'll have to make yourself. Keep your limitations in mind. If it's not a life-threatening felony (a suspect drawing a gun in a convenience store with you in line, a drive-by shooting aimed directly at you, or some other murderous action), you may just want to call for help, observe, and gather as much information as you can. Never put your family at risk; it's just not worth it. Also, as in the beating scenario, think about the negative impact on your spouse or young son or daughter if you get into a shouting/screaming match with some jerk. Do you really want your loved ones to see you in a physical confrontation like that?

Decide if you really need to get involved or if you should just drop into your supplemental role as an expert professional witness. The latter should be your only course of action if you've been drinking, even a little. No officer wants to have a deep discussion with a defense attorney about his or her relative sobriety level on the day of an incident, especially if it involved cars or firearms.

As one veteran patrol supervisor puts it, "There is no law that says you have to take action during a crime. You may have a moral obligation to act, but you don't have any legal obligation to put yourself in jeopardy off-duty. Be aware of your limitations in terms of equipment and self-protection. You and your family come first."

You should make any decision to act during an off-duty confrontation under these guidelines: "I want to protect myself and my family from physical harm. I want to protect myself and my family from civil harm. I will take any steps I feel necessary to do both." Off-duty confrontations are on the rise. Use your good judgment and remember that your safety is more important than anything that happens out there.

Orcutt Police Nunchakus: A New Defensive Control Weapon

The police profession faces an ever-changing world. Just as our society is becoming more sophisticated, it's also becoming more violent. Police departments must rise to meet these changes or face an increasing number of control problems.

In terms of changes and advancements in police operations, few topics generate more discussion than officer-safety equipment. Pick up any major law-enforcement publication, and you'll probably see a lengthy article discussing the merits of semiautos over revolvers, side-handled batons over straight sticks, the use of metal "wrist-gripping" tools to gain pain compliance, or some similar exchange concerning future advancements in officer safety and equipment use.

One such discussion now sweeping through police circles concerns the use (and abuse) of a new tool that is not without controversy: the police nunchaku.

We've all seen these weapons in martial-arts and adventure movies. It looks like two pieces of hard wood joined together by a short piece of cord. In the right hands, it's a deadly weapon. In the wrong hands, it's probably a felony just to carry it. From the karate studio and the movie screen

cer go through an eight-hour refresher course each year to supplement his or her current skills. While police nunchaku weapons like the Orcutt model still must prove their worth to both the police and the public, their presence illustrates the constant changes we're seeing in officer safety and tactics. Time, additional research, and a careful evaluation process will decide whether the police nunchaku has a place in police work.

Outlaw Biker
Stops

Motorcycle riding is a popular activity in this country. Many people own motorcycles ranging in size, shape, and price from huge "GoldWing" touring models to off-road dirt bikes. Most motorcyclists are law-abiding folks who just enjoy riding along the open road. But another category of riders exists, one that is not particularly interested in obeying the law or even being classified with other motorcyclists. I'm referring to the "outlaw" bikers.

Over the years, our outlaw biker population seems to have evolved. During the 1960s and 1970s, we saw the hard-core outlaw bent on stomping "citizens" and offending everyone with tales of rape, pillage, and beer swilling. The 19?0s and 1990s groups are known for other endeavors, like the creation and sale of crystal methamphetamine.

That's not to say they like cops any better than their older counterparts. Rest assured, all outlaw bikers dislike cops. They still think of themselves as the only real Americans.

While the days of outlaw biker-sponsored community terror are over most large cities, you never know when you'll run across one out on the road. Sheriffs' departments, state highway patrols, and various state and federal rangers usually have their hands full when these roving

◀

"patriots" decide to make one of their patented Labor or Memorial Day runs to local campgrounds.

You should automatically know that you're dealing with a potentially dangerous person, but here are a few tactical reminders to consider with "outlaw" biker types.

• Get a cover unit. Some of these people are chronic meth users, which makes them unpredictable, prone to extreme violence, and very antipolice. Get another officer to cover you, preferably prior to the stop. You don't want to fight 250 pounds of leather-covered meth freak by yourself.

• In a strange sort of paradox, these people respect authority, so don't be afraid to take command of the situation immediately. They look for weakness in officers, especially when riding in groups. Watch for the bigmouths who try to cause a confrontation by taunting you.

• Female officers must use extreme caution, as outlaw bikers will want to challenge their authority during any stop. This chauvinistic behavior can lead to a rapid physical confrontation if you don't take control early on. Give simple, firm commands and stand your ground.

• Stay to the right of the suspect's handlebars. Have him kill the engine on his bike. Position yourself so that he has to talk to you over his right shoulder; most people fight, stab, and shoot with their right hands and carry weapons accordingly so it's safer for you to be on that side (it's also curbside for you). Make him stay on the bike, with the kickstand up.

• Do an immediate visual pat-down followed by a hands-on search for weapons and contraband. These people are *always armed* with something, usually a sheath knife on their belts. In some cases, they will also carry boot knives, heavy wrenches, tire irons, or even handguns in shoulder holster rigs. They also like to wear large chains as belts, so keep their hands away from their waistbands. Watch for signs that the outlaw biker is wearing body armor. This should quickly tell you you're dealing with a confirmed bad guy.

• Search carefully. These people like to wear many layers of bulky clothes, including heavy Levi or leather jackets and similar heavy-duty pants and boots. They're usually quite familiar with regular police stops and will use many creative hiding places to protect their stashes. You may have to dig through layers of filthy clothes to find dope or weapons, so wear gloves and don't miss anything.

• Some officers like to get outlaw bikers off their "hogs" for any citation or field interview. The thought behind this is sometimes the bike itself is a rolling weapon, i.e., possibly holding knives, guns, bombs, or even hidden ignition systems that allow the rider to start the bike without a key and escape.

• If you do have the suspect climb off his machine, you may want to use it as a barrier to keep him at a distance. After a pat-down, conduct all your business (passing paperwork, etc.) over the bike or in some cases, the hood of your car.

• Using good Contact & Cover procedures, have your partner keep the suspect away from his bike while you examine it carefully for any noticeable weapons, contraband, or equipment violations.

• Always look for signs of drug use, especially methamphetamine. These people live and die for crystal. It's always on or in their bodies. Look hard for dilated pupils, excessive nervousness, nasal damage, high pulse rate, sweating, and other similar symptoms of meth abuse.

• Be sure to run the vehicle as soon as you make the stop. In some cities, motorcycle "chop shops" are legendary. Run the Vehicle Identification Number and make sure it matches the registration card. Switched, stolen, or missing plates or VIN numbers are an immediate clue that you're dealing with a hard-core suspect. Send your field interview information to your auto theft section if you think the biker is involved in stolen parts and bikes.

• Dig deep with these people. One veteran officer who works with outlaw bikers on a regular basis makes it a point to always tow their bikes if he finds any legal reason to do so. Check for license status and class, traffic warrants, and insurance. Inspect the bike for road hazards or safety violations and cite away. These might include: no turn signals, a missing or broken speedometer, or unsafe tires or handlebars. Traffic officers can often give you good motorcycle cite sections.

• Get good FI information for your narcotics, property, and organized crime detectives. Outlaw bikers like to move quantities of drugs and stolen parts or property. Take photos if you can.

• Outlaw biker women can be just as dangerous as their male counterparts. Because they know cops are usually reluctant to search females, these bikers often load their women up with dope and guns for safekeeping. Be advised that these women will fight as hard as any man if provoked.

• Be careful not to insult the suspect about his bike or his "colors" if he's wearing them. These are hard-earned, hard-fought tools of glory for these people. Manhandling a biker's colors would be akin to having a suspect remove your badge and bend it. Dropping a biker's colors is cause for a serious, serious fight. That's not to say you should treat these people like royalty, just that their perception of their colors relates to their worth, value, and identity. Don't poke sticks into hornet nests.

• Another irritating factor about dealing with outlaw bikers is their total lack of fear of the law. These people truly don't care about you or what you're saying to them. Threatening them with jail is like swimming upstream. You'll get nowhere quickly. In conversations, these guys have said, "Jail? Go ahead! It just gives me a break from my bills and my old lady."

• If you're going to make an arrest, get enough cover and do it. Save the speeches that you use on the Yes and Maybe people. Outlaw bikers are definitely No people. Be careful with them and make the arrest as quickly as possible. Impound their bikes if you can, process them, and get them to jail.

Handling bikers during traffic stops and other contacts is no different than any other potentially high-risk encounter. Use good safety habits, get ample cover, and offer strong command presence throughout the stop.

separately around each ankle and hooked together to prevent a foot chase, and in the hog-tie position.

Another restraining device that came about after the rise in PCP use is the nylon capture net. While the capture net works well in the right situations—for PCP users or mentally unstable suspects—it is not as portable as the other two devices.

The capture net takes time to set up and requires at least four trained officers to use it properly. Officers called to a scene with a violent suspect must quickly decide if they can use the capture net. It usually rides in a patrol car trunk in a large gear bag and works much like a fishing net. Two officers use long aluminum poles and, in some cases, a small dry-chemical fire extinguisher to distract the suspect and lead him into an area where the other two officers can throw the net on him. This part is critical, as the officers using the net must be able to contain the suspect before throwing it.

The two officers holding the nylon net lines stand apart from each other and rush the suspect at the same time. They throw the weighted net over his head and move quickly away from him. Each of their lines closes the net tightly around the suspect, and this usually knocks him to the ground. Other officers can move in to handcuff and control the suspect before removing the net.

Each of these three restraining devices represents new and practical thinking from law-enforcement equipment designers. Each one is now commonly used because today's police officers need to control potentially dangerous suspects quickly and effectively.

Positioning

You see it time and time again—officers standing next to traffic violators with their guns perilously close to itchy hands. How many times have you driven by a traffic stop in progress, only to see the officer explaining something to a person with his or her gun side only inches away from possible danger?

It seems that since we make so many routine stops, we sometimes forget the basic FI stance, which was designed entirely for our safety. Besides the obvious gun protection/retention advantages it offers, it also gives you a good balance point if you need to defend yourself. Used properly, the FI position allows you to drop everything and control a suspect who may be trying to knock you off balance. Your feet are well spaced, your weight is evenly distributed (40 percent on your front foot and 60 percent on your back foot), your gun is away from unwanted hands, and your baton ring is forward.

The FI stance is easy and practical, yet some officers only use it selectively, depending on the situation. This is foolish. Use it all the time, regardless of whether you feel threatened or not. It is a good habit to practice.

Some officers use it only on obvious dirtbags but not

Practice! Practice! Practice! Know Your Equipment

When was the last time you used your Mace—either on a suspect or aimed at the ground to test it? When was the last time you even reached for it?

I'll admit it's not a common tool. Few situations warrant its use, but it's still nice to know you have it on your belt. The point of this is simple: practice with your stuff. Just because you haven't used a particular tool for months doesn't mean you shouldn't constantly train with it. You may clean your gun every week and practice with it often, but what about the rest of your equipment?

Scientists have conducted exhaustive studies on our ability to retain certain skills. For some task or movement to become an ingrained habit, we've learned that on the average, we must perform a task at least 3,500 times before it becomes burned into our memory. Think about how this relates to the movements involved in police work. Repetition is the key to developing what is known as "muscle-memory." In high-stress situations, you will automatically revert to how you trained yourself to do something.

Defensive tactics instructors know this. It's why you pulled your gun so many times in the academy, why you practiced those arrest-and-control handholds until your wrists felt like they were broken, and why you swung that baton around so much.

You may remember the story of the California Highway Patrol officer who was shot by an approaching suspect while he reloaded his service revolver. The officer was killed as he put his empty brass in his pocket—just as he was taught to do. In that pressure shooting situation, he reverted back to his training. Obviously, it was a fatal mistake, and it led to some significant changes in the way we reload our weapons in combat situations.

Here's another example that drives this point home: if you've ever been near an ongoing shooting situation, it's amazing how you never even notice that you've pulled your gun. Instinct and training take over, and you react accordingly. These are the same instincts that allow you to grab the suspect's wrists (or neck) in just the right manner to make an arrest.

As good as you think you may be at certain police-related tactics, you must remember that training and constant practice are the keys to keeping your skills sharp. Even Special Weapons & Tactics (SWAT) members, who are surely the most qualified and well-trained members of any police department, practice constantly with their tools, weapons, defensive tactics, and approach techniques.

The bottom line is that you should be extremely familiar with your equipment before you even get out of your patrol car. To help you achieve that aim, here are a few suggestions.

Handguns

Your departmental range is the best place ~~is a ou~~ our firearms skills.

- Don't just take those practice ~~plink away~~ at the target. Concentrate on w~~ou're doing and~~

set up a thorough training regimen.

- Dry-fire to improve your wrist and finger strength.
- Shoot only three rounds in the cylinder to break that "clenching the trigger" habit.
- Shoot left-handed (or right-handed if you're a lefty).
- Practice your reloading (with your eyes closed), point shooting, barricade shooting, and kneeling shots, just like you would if you were involved in a high-risk vehicle stop.
- Visiting the range once a month is just not enough to stay sharp. Go often and practice efficiently. The seconds you shave off your techniques may make the difference in saving your life.

Handcuffing

When was the last time you used the "felony-kneeling" handcuff technique? Probably not in quite awhile. Most arrests either use the FBI cuffing technique or the famous "rolling-on-the-ground-with-three-other-officers" technique. Just like you should be able to shoot with either hand, you should be able to reach the handcuffs on your belt with either hand. What if your primary hand were injured?

- Place your cuffs in the center of your back, where you can get to them in any position.
- Keep your spare cuffs in an accessible location as well.
- Grab your partner and spend some off-duty time practicing the FBI, felony-kneeling, prone, and high-risk cuffing techniques. Also, spend some time practicing come-alongs with either arm, the wrist twists, and the other takedowns you need to control violent suspects. (Be careful with these; no one wants to go on light duty for practicing too roughly.)

Baton

If you're lucky, your department will provide karate bags at several convenient locations for you to practice your baton blows, blocks, and swings. If you can't make use of a karate bag at your station, then consider buying one for home use. These bags are relatively inexpensive ($50 or less if you can get a used one), and they really help you get the feel of your stick. Hit the thing every day you work, even if it's just for a few minutes.

Spend some time at least once per week thoroughly practicing with your baton. If you use the PR-24 model, run through all of the draws (rear draw included), the chops, the blocks, and, of course, the striking spins. If you use a straight stick, practice those chops, U-turns, strokes, blocks, and power swings. After a short time, you should be able to give yourself a quick test in baton techniques each time you train with it.

Mace, Flashlight, Sap, Cord-Cuff Restraint, and Kubotan

- Test your Mace at least once every other month. Make sure it sits securely on your belt and you can reach it quickly.

- Practice using your flashlight as a baton; you never know when you may be out of the car without your stick and may need to protect yourself.

- If you can carry an authorized sap, keep it in a handy pocket or pouch and practice with the various striking techniques.

- Keep your cord-cuff in a handy pocket or pouch and practice with each of the three restraining techniques: the around-the-waist restraint, the around-the-ankles restraint, and the hog-tie (see pages 22-24 for more information).

- If you carry the popular Kubotan "Persuader" key-ring stick, then you need to know how to use the device correctly. Practice the come-alongs, blocks, and strikes that make this small device so effective.

Self-Defense Techniques

Just because you may not have the time or inclination to take a martial-arts class doesn't mean that you cannot keep these skills honed. There are a few techniques you can practice at home.

- In front of a stand-up mirror, you can practice quick shin and kneecap kicks and perfect those short, close-range punches to the chest, ribs, and sternum.
- Practice hand-to-hand fighting from a variety of balanced stances, including the FI stance.
- If you really want to get good, have some fellow officers who are skilled at martial arts give you some pointers.
- Again, you may want to consider buying that karate bag for your home. This way, you can practice baton and hand fighting techniques in your spare time. (No more excuses!)

Weapons Retention

Get with a partner and work on these critical (and life-saving) techniques.

- Gun retention begins with the proper equipment. If you're still hanging onto that old holster for sentimental reasons, it's time to get rid of it before it kills you. Many officers killed in the line of duty were shot with their own weapons.

- Keeping your weapon requires the proper "bladed" stance that keeps your gun away from the crook you're facing.
- A strong grip will keep your gun in its proper place—in your hands and not in those of your suspect.
- Lastly, keep this critical point in mind as you train: your enemy is out there practicing, too. Street hoods, convicts in prison, and the standard assortment of dopers and nuts you see on your beat are all out there trying things they hope will give them an edge. I've talked to crooks who know more about weapons retention, escapes, and firearms than we do. This is not a pleasant thought to consider.

To drive this point home, remember this sobering thought: every day you put off practicing these defensive techniques and tactics is another day lost. Your enemy is practicing, and he will improve his edge if you give him the opportunity. The more you train and the more you practice, the better chance you'll have in a pressure-filled moment.

In stressful situations, your body will attempt to protect itself by reverting to what it knows how to do. Practice is the key to success and survival in this job. Don't just strap on that belt and go to work. Practice!

are people on most police departments who are paid to tell things to the media. Let them do their job.

As one longtime police press spokesman so succinctly puts it, "Remember, when you're talking to a reporter, there is no such thing as being 'off-the-record.' If you have any contact with the media, let us handle it. We deal with these people every day, and we know them."

Repeat: if you have any dealings with the media that make you uncomfortable, refer them to your immediate supervisor or a press information officer at the scene. It's their job to cut through all the accusatory questioning and similar garbage and give out only the pertinent information.

The best rule of thumb is: if you don't know, don't guess; and if you do know, don't say anything until it's been cleared through the chain of command. Let the press-relations officers and the supervisors do their part to get you off the hook if you are unsure of yourself. Further, if you are ever harassed, bothered at home, or approached by a media person in what you feel is an improper manner, make sure someone hears about it.

I know there are some television and newspaper people who are supportive of law enforcement, so it's not fair to lump them all together. But if the articles in the local papers and the letters to the editors are any indication of our current popularity with the media, it's no wonder we feel defensive.

In the interest of enhancing our image as professionals, we need to regard the media as the mongoose regards the cobra—very carefully.

Prisoner Control

My current theory surrounding rehabilitative penology—or what to do with crooks in jail—centers around my belief that these people have far too much free time on their hands.

Witness the disclosure from the Franklin County Sheriff's office concerning jail inmates in the city of Columbus, Ohio. It seems that while these fine citizens traveled from one jail to another in the county prisoner vans, they discovered a way to break their handcuff chains.

According to an article in *Crime Control Digest* quoting Sheriff Earl Smith, "When the deputy opened the back of the van, all ten guys were smiling and said, 'See what we did?' Each prisoner held up his arms to show broken handcuffs."

Apparently the inmates learned they could wedge the handcuff chain through a slotted hole in their seat-belt buckles. By jamming the chain into this slot and twisting it quickly, the inmates were able to shear off the handcuff chain where it attached to the cuff itself.

This Ohio sheriff adds that once the inmates were back in the main jail, they wasted no time telling the other crooks about this cuff-breaking procedure.

We've all seen or heard stories of drug-crazies with superhuman strength snapping handcuffs behind their backs like Hercules. This tells you something you should already know: handcuffs do not provide total security. They can be broken or picked by all but the stupidest of crooks. You should never rely on handcuffs alone for total prisoner security. Some of these people have been in cuffs more times than you and I have had birthdays. Cuffs are only a temporary restraining tool.

Effective prisoner control begins as soon as the cuffs are on the suspect's wrists. He or she becomes your immediate responsibility. You have to protect yourself from the prisoner, and you have a legal duty to protect the prisoner from harm while that person is in your custody. Once you turn your prisoner over to the jail administrators, prisoner control becomes their worry. But until then, here are a few reminders to help you achieve your goals:

• Remember to double-lock your handcuffs as soon as it's safe and the arrest situation is over.

• Search suspects carefully. Veteran crooks often conceal actual or homemade handcuff keys in strange and mysterious places. Always assume your prisoner may have a key somewhere. Find it before it finds you.

• Monitor the level of bellyaching from your prisoners about how tight the cuffs feel on their wrists. Make a point to check blood circulation and make adjustments if necessary. Be sure to document that you checked the cuffs in your arrest report. One or two sentences on paper could save you from a phony civil-rights-violation lawsuit later.

• Use your cord-cuff restraint. It's an important tool at your disposal. By looping it around the suspect's waist and fastening the hook to the cuff chain, you can prevent any Houdini-like gyrations in the back of your car. Few things chill your soul like the sight of your prisoner fishing for a match to light the cigarette he just shoved between his lips.

• Don't be shy about using the cord-cuff to restrain violent, psychotic, or drugged prisoners. It only takes a few seconds—with the help of another officer—and it can save you from explaining a broken rear windshield or dented doors. Again, make sure you document your use of the hog-tie restraint in your arrest report. If you're afraid the suspect may injure himself, you, or your car, use the cord-cuff restraint.

• If you're transporting only one prisoner to jail, put him or her on the right side of the cage. You can angle your rear-view mirror slightly to watch for trouble, and it may prevent the old spitting-on-the-head routine.

• If you're working alone and park at your station, ask another officer to watch your prisoner while you go inside. It's not always possible, but try to find someone. For better visibility, leave the dome light on to illuminate the inside of your car.

• Practice strict officer-safety habits when moving your prisoner to and from any blood-draw or Intoxilizer facilities. Remind this person of the need to follow your explicit instructions. Watch the prisoner constantly and protect your weapon at all times.

• Be especially careful in the rest-room area during the collection of urine samples. Have another officer hold your gun outside the rest room and listen through the door while you talk to your prisoner. Uncuff one hand and immediately cuff the other to his belt. After the suspect gives the sample, ask him to set it on to the toilet and then recuff him. Then, wearing rubber gloves, cap the bottle and impound it. God help you if some drunk grabs your gun in the bathroom. Protect your weapon!

• U.S. Marshals Service studies show that an officer's personal stress level is often high during and immediately after the actual arrest. It usually goes down once the officer begins the booking process. However, the suspect's blood pressure and adrenaline levels often rise dramatically just prior to his or her arrival at the jail. The fear of going inside may cause your prisoner to try something irrational. Keep your guard up all the way to the jail door.

• Remember to take immediate control of your prisoner

as soon as he or she is out of the car. You may want to hold the cuff chain, the cord cuff, or even apply a wristlock to prevent an escape or an assault.

• Practice good officer-safety habits when you're inside the jail intake area, too. When you're in the jail room alone or with another officer and his or her suspect, never remove your handcuffs until the last possible moment. The two suspects may decide to fight if both of them are out of cuffs. It's always easier to take them off than it is to put them on.

• Leave the cuffs in place until the booking process begins and watch each prisoner carefully. Keep them facing forward and explain the intake rules. Save the chitchat with other officers until after your crook is on the other side of the bars.

Give some thought to your own prisoner control methods. Following good officer safety habits will protect you and your prisoner from harm.

Radio Awareness

"One twenty-three King, I'm a half block from the bomb threat sce—" (BOOM! Loud explosion, followed by dead silence over the air). We all know from films at the academy that a portable radio can trigger an explosive device if it's used too close to the scene. As far as I know, this scenario hasn't happened lately, but that doesn't mean it couldn't. This frightening thought should help you remember that at all times radio awareness is critical to your safety, your partner's safety, and the lives of innocent people around you.

Using the radio correctly is also important for other scenarios involving electrical equipment, not just with bomb threats. As an example, according to studies on drunk-driving arrests, using your radio too close to the testing room may interfere with the Intoxilizer. You know defense attorneys already know this, so don't make the mistake of using your portable near these areas unless it's an emergency.

In any situation where the information needs to remain a secret—like a bomb threat—remember to use the telephone. If you get a desk call to tell someone a family member has died, don't get on the air and announce that information when you arrive at the scene. This holds true for simulate field conditions as closely as possible. If you get in a gun fight, chances are you'll be wearing these items. Why not give yourself every training edge? You're trying to create "muscle memory" between your mind and body. Under stressful conditions, your body will react as it was trained. Good habits during training lead to life-saving habits in the field. Get busy! Those rounds are waiting.

l

gi
pa
has
O
shalt
quenc
ing to r

Read and Learn

While sorting through my junk mail, I came across an interesting catalog from a knife company. Inside, I saw page after page of belt knives, throwing knives, fighting knives, attack knives, commando knives, boot knives, daggers, bayonets, machetes, sword canes and umbrellas, stilettos, battle axes, and even straight razors. You get the point. If it's sharp and deadly, you can buy it from this catalog. You can even buy a number of different books explaining how to throw, sharpen, or fight with your new toys.

Seeing these weapons from the safety of the catalog will help you recognize them in the field, which is the real value of reading catalogs, booklets, and magazines about those things. The old saying, "Forewarned is forearmed," is especially true in police work. Knowing what the bad guys are up to can give you an excellent tactical advantage.

One of the best places to learn about new weapons and neighborhood bad-guy tactics is at your local bookstore or magazine stand. Outlaw biker, karate, and survivalist magazines are filled with interesting information a savvy cop can use for his or her own protection.

Want to see the latest in martial-arts weaponry? Pick up a copy of a karate or kung fu magazine and read the adver-

Spanish Lessons: Slang from the Streets

Uncovering good information on the streets can lead you to felony arrests, help you cancel cases, and protect you and your partner from assaults.

To use this kind of information effectively, you need the ability to decipher what you hear on the street from citizens, witnesses, victims, and your own snitches. If it's in English, it's usually no problem to translate street talk into something useful. But what if these conversations are in Spanish? The information may be just as valuable, but if you aren't bilingual and can't understand it, what good does it do you?

"Why should I care," you may say, "I don't work in a Spanish-speaking area." Think again. With Mexico on our border and a rapidly growing Hispanic population in our country, it makes sense for police officers to learn as much Spanish as possible.

A case in point: working in San Ysidro, California, I've arrested a number of Mexican street and prison gang members for everything from dope to warrants to urinating in public and possession of weapons.

One night I pinched two gang members and took them uptown. En route to jail, I heard them carry on a whispered conversation in Spanish. I listened carefully and extracted enough to realize that they were planning to try to either jump me or escape when we reached the jail entrance.

After arriving at jail, I used a come-along wrist lock to remove the first prisoner from my car before he could twist away. I pulled the second suspect out the same way and prevented any problems. You could tell by their faces they looked surprised that they missed their opportunity to fight or run.

The point is I picked up enough of the conversation to realize that something bad was probably about to happen. I took Spanish classes in college, so I had a distinct advantage over someone with no training. But what might have happened if I didn't know what those gangsters were planning?

Many local community colleges in your area offer beginning Spanish courses throughout the year. The cost is quite low and you can usually fit the hours around your work schedule. You'll be amazed to see how fast you can pick up the language after just a few weeks of concentrated study.

In the meantime, I'll include a list of common street Spanish terms often used by gang members and others who are "in the mix." This is hardly the ultimate guide to the Spanish language, but you may hear these on a regular basis. If you can memorize a few of them, it may help you on the job.

You may have heard none of these or all of them. Some of them are common; others are not so well known. In any case, you may want to write each word or phrase on a 3" x 5" note card—Spanish on one side, English on the other— to help you remember them.

Birria, Pisto—beer, booze
Calmate—calm down!
Camarada—friend, associate
Carcancha—junky car
Carnal, Carnala—brother, sister
El Condado—county jail

Chale—no
Chiva—heroin
Chota—police
Chuco, Pachuco—gang veteran, gangster
Chuntaros, Mujados—aliens
Chupar, Dorar—to smoke or cook as with heroin
Chanates, Mayates, Piñas, Tintos—black people
Ese—hey or hey, man
Farmero—prison gang member
Filia, Filero—knife
Frajos—cigarettes
Gavachos—white people
Grifa, Mota, Yierba, Sacate—marijuana
Hay Te Wacho—see you later
Huevon—lazy (often a gang member's nickname)
Marranos—pigs/cops
Menso—idiot (often a gang member's nickname)
Mosca—fly, pest (often a gang member's nickname)
Movidas—gang rules
Orale—hey, okay, or right on
Paca—gang fight
Pastillas—pills
Pinta, Pinto—prison, ex-con
Pistola—gun
Puntas, Clavos—needles
"Que Gacho"—a bad scene
Rata, Relaje—rat, snitch
Rafa, Rifamos—rule, we rule
Simon—yeah
Talco—cocaine
Tonto—stupid (often a gang member's nickname)
Torcida, Torcido—locked up, busted
Truca—watch out
Vida Loca—this crazy life

These are just a few words, expressions, and slang phrases used by some Hispanic gang members and other street people. For more help, consider taking a Spanish course. In the meantime, meet with some Spanish-speaking officers in your agency and learn some of the more common terms heard in your jails and on the streets. Make it a point to listen to Spanish conversations on the streets or in the back of your patrol car. Your knowledge of the language could save your life.

Street Awareness: Using Tips to Catch Crooks

A man lies sleeping on a motel bed in El Centro, California. His roommates sit watching a TV show called "America's Most Wanted." Suddenly, they see a photo of their friend appear on the screen. Their dozing companion is wanted for murder in Louisiana. The roommates quietly sneak off to the manager's office to use the phone. In minutes, El Centro Police arrive, point several dozen guns at the man lying on the bed, and arrest him for his outstanding felony warrants.

A true story? Yes. What's the point? You never know who you might stumble across. This holds especially true for members of the police profession. The history of the American fugitive from justice is filled with stories of cops happening upon Mr. Wanted in the most common of places.

Remember the New Jersey State Trooper who stopped and arrested a member of a Japanese terrorist organization? Another trooper in New England stopped some Arab terrorists driving a van full of explosives. Clearly, you can never predict who you might run into on your beat.

Information is critical to the police officer's daily law-enforcement chores. Your ability to locate and arrest suspects is only as good as the information you receive. This information comes from a variety of different sources, including: lineup discussions, crime series updates, memos from detectives (also known as Investigative Supplementals), the FBI Top Ten List, and, most importantly, your contacts on the street.

Some officers make it a habit to bring a pack of cigarettes with them into the field, even if they don't smoke. Better than money, cigarettes can be a powerful bargaining weapon. You'd be amazed at the number of street hoods who would give up their own grandmother for a few nicotine sticks.

The terminology in your area may be different, i.e., BOLs (Be on the Lookout), ATLs (Attempt To Locate), All-Units Advisories, etc. However you refer to these kinds of information sheets isn't important; just remember that the piece of paper is a valuable resource for you in the field.

Two of these information sources—detective memos (or BOLs, etc.) and the FBI Top Ten List—sometimes get short shrift from officers in the field.

Some officers are diligent, keeping track of their paperwork in a small notebook and reading each new suspect description as it appears. Still other officers actively seek out the suspects wanted by the detectives and routinely bring in good quality lineup photos, prints, and FIs.

Unfortunately, other officers barely glance at the suspect description reports and don't bother to keep track of them either. This last habit is both careless and unsafe. It's careless because not keeping a current supply of suspect descriptions handy in your patrol car is like throwing away good probable cause for your FIs. It's unsafe because you could contact one of the listed suspects and not even know he or she is known to be armed and dangerous.

The information provided in the narratives of your BOLs or Investigative Supplementals gives you the necessary reasons to make contact with potential suspects—whether or not they are on your beat.

Some officers only give the BOLs/Investigative

Supplementals a cursory look, unless the listed crimes or suspects reside in their division or beat. This habit is short-sighted, especially since most good crooks have cars or can take public transportation from their homes to their favorite stomping grounds.

Just because the crime took place in one area of your city doesn't mean the suspects may not live, work, or "case" in another. Read the descriptions and think about how the crimes and suspects from other areas may eventually creep into your own division.

If your agency publishes Crime Series Updates, you can also focus your attention on specific beat problems. They may also list tools or weapons used and very detailed suspect actions to help you pinpoint your crook.

From a safety standpoint, you need to know as much about your enemy as possible. If you know your suspect used a knife, a shotgun, or a baseball bat in all of his crimes, you can be better equipped to handle him if you should meet.

Further, the BOLs/Investigative Supplementals may also list the suspect's tattoos, scars, hangouts, gang affiliation, parole status, and other helpful identifiers. While this information will certainly help you locate and identify the suspect, it may also save your skin. Heed the old police adage, "Forewarned is forearmed."

The safety aspect holds especially true when dealing with the illustrious members of the FBI Top Ten list. Here we find the worst of the worst, the veritable scum of the earth. Knowing about each subject's tendencies, habits, and appearances can be the key to a safe arrest.

I realize the photos are often fuzzy and the information may not be entirely complete, but you can always call the agent assigned to the case for more details. As the members of your own Major Crimes Units will gladly tell you, it's possible to run across a wanted crook in the most common of places, e.g., the supermarket, a convenience store, or a fast-food stand.

Read all of the information that comes from various

sources around your department. Talk to other officers, supervisors, and detectives around you. Study the BOLs/Investigative Supplementals and the Top Ten lists as they appear and keep track of the people listed on them. Remember to update the supplementals by cancelling the cases that are longer current (suspect in custody, etc.).

The more information you have, the easier (and the safer) your job becomes. Who knows? You may come across a major felony suspect just around the next corner.

A National City, California, detective arrested a multi-case "hot prowl" rapist after the suspect walked by him in a motel parking lot. Do your homework. It could pay off in a big arrest.

Stress Control through Breath Control

Besides teaching you many things about other people—like what's wrong with them—police work can also tell you a few things about yourself. My response to a recent high-risk radio call gave me some interesting insights into my own physiological limitations.

During an ice-cold graveyard shift we received a call to deal with a known mental patient on drugs. He was high on crystal meth, threatening his mother, and tearing up her house. Four of us arrived and went inside to confront this highly enraged person. We found him in a back bedroom, armed with a razor. He attempted to run past us and the struggle was on.

We spent the better part of nearly three minutes on top of this frightened, powerful guy. He was trying very diligently to lift three of us off of his frame so he could either fight or escape. With help from one officer's Orcutt Police Nunchakus on the suspect's right wrist and much twisting and pulling from myself and another good-sized cop on his left, we finally got him into handcuffs.

Any time longer than one minute is a long time to fight a drug-bent, wide-eyed, two-hundred-pound wildman. During the struggle, I was on the suspect's back yelling,

"STOP FIGHTING!" into his ear. After he was restrained by the handcuffs, we used a cord-cuff restraint to keep him from kicking us.

From the house, two of us had to carry him to the car, a trip that felt like the Bataan Death March; this boy was heavy. He kept twisting around like a python inside a burlap bag.

Once he was safely inside the car, I stopped to regroup. I found myself literally gasping for air. I felt like someone was standing with a foot on each lung. Finally, I caught my breath and could continue. I remember being surprised at how physically tired I was when I got home that morning. I slept longer than usual and woke up feeling like forty miles of bad road.

Some of you out there may be thinking, "Why didn't you use the Police Department-approved Kansas City Vascular Restraint Technique?" (Or a word that rhymes with "broke.") Don't think I didn't consider it, but the suspect was face down on a thick comforter and the room was far too small to move him anywhere but the bed. Another example of "might having to make right."

Nearly one month after this call, I took an advanced karate belt test at my studio. I knew all of the necessary techniques and felt comfortable with my fitness level. These tests are always highly charged events for me because of the ceremony and ritual involved, not to mention the fear of embarrassment or the wrath of my instructor if I fail.

The test went well up until the end when I had to do a long set of kicking drills up and down the mat. By that point, I had similar feelings to what I had during the mental patient radio call: very heavy exhale breathing, a slight sense of light-headedness, and an inability to catch my breath.

I managed to gasp through the drills and pass the test. Afterward I thought, "What's going on?" I trained hard for this, ran at night, rode my bike for miles, sweated all over the treadmill, climbed stairs, and played racquetball. I burned my lungs for what seemed like endless hours. My wind was good. Why did I feel that way?

The answer came from my karate instructor. After the test he said, "Do you know you hyperventilate when you do your techniques? I can see you taking short, fast breaths followed by long, deep exhales. That's why you ran out of gas toward the end."

A phone call to my partner revealed basically the same problem on the night of the big wrestling match. Heavy breathing under extreme exertion.

I'm in decent cardiovascular shape; so what was the common factor in each of these two incidents? Stress.

When I jog or ride my bike, no one is trying to hurt or judge me. I set my own pace and adjust my comfort zone as necessary. Police work and the inherent rise and fall of strenuous, occasionally terrifying activity doesn't let you set a comfort zone. You can't control the "spikes" in your stress level because you simply can't predict when they'll occur.

But while you can't predict the future—or know when the next high-stress episode is imminent—you can adjust your physical self to create a more controlled reaction.

We know from our own experiences that during high-stress situations we tend to breathe at a fast and shallow rate. This can create a kind of vicious circle (as in my examples), where the more you breathe the more your body craves air. To beat this craving for oxygen, you have to send your body a different signal. You can break this stress cycle by breathing in an opposite fashion: slow and deep, with control.

Easy to say and hard to do? Yes. Am I telling you to relearn something you do more than 20,000 times per day? Yes. It's not easy, and it demands mental and physical discipline. I've been practicing it now for several months and on rare occasions I still find myself reverting back to my old shallow-breath habits.

There are literally dozens of deep-breathing techniques that can help you during a high-stress encounter. SWAT teams use what they call "SWAT breathing" to control themselves during the obviously high-stress encounters they face.

By consciously controlling your breathing, you can take your mind off your body's needs to concentrate on the tactical matters at hand. I'll explain several different techniques, and you can choose from them.

- *The 4-4-4 method*—With this technique, you inhale through your nose to the mental count of four, hold your breath to the mental count of four, and exhale through your mouth to the mental count of four. This is especially effective for those moments just before a high-stress activity, like when you're in the car heading to a hairy call.

- *The 1-2-1 method*—Using this technique, you breathe in steadily through your nose as one long count, hold your breath for a two count, and then exhale through your mouth for one long count. This is a method used by many sniper and pistol team shooters.

- *Belly breathing*—This method centers your breathing on your abdomen and your diaphragm. Using your belly, you can control the flow of air into your lungs by inhaling and exhaling at a slow, rhythmic pace. Most of us are chest breathers when we should be belly breathers.

- *If you suspect symptoms of hyperventilation*, cup your hands around your mouth and exhale into them. This will trap your exhaled breath and balance your carbon dioxide and oxygen levels. (Some people breathe into a paper bag for the same effect, but you risk looking ridiculous.)

Before you put this kind of stress control aside as more New Age BS, consider the fact that cops who can control their bodies are able to think more clearly than cops who can't. You're paid to make the right decision, but you have to be in control before you can make it. Stressful situations can put our bodies in a "shutdown" mode as a form of self-protection. We can't afford to shut down in the streets. Breathe! But do it with control.

Stress Warning Signs

An issue of the Dallas Police paper *The Shield* caught my eye. They reprinted a comprehensive list of law enforcement "warning signs," and since *Streetwork* is designed to protect the inner you as well as the outer you, I think the list deserves some discussion.

Some of these signs are easy to recognize; others are more subtle. Some of them you may see in yourself, while others may only come to your attention after some internal conversation with yourself, or some pointed discussions with your family, your partner, your peers, or even your supervisors.

Read over the list and the short explanations to see how they may relate to how you feel about yourself and this job. If you find yourself saying, "Uh oh, some of this sounds like me," then maybe you need to evaluate your present stress level.

Help can come from various sources, the best of which is from psychological counseling, if it's available. You can also get help from peers, marriage and family counselors, and stress-control books and audiotapes. (At the end, I'll provide the name of an excellent stress-relief tape designed especially for law-enforcement officers.)

Here are some of the key stress-related signs, as they relate directly to law enforcement officers:

1. *Change of personality*—You're moody, aggressive, and emotional. You may feel like you're on a roller-coaster ride emotionally; up one day and down the next. People around you may notice you aren't your usual cheery self.

2. *Change in personal appearance*—You feel as if you just don't give a damn. Your appearance and looks start to become less important. You may have problems with your skin, hair, teeth, bleeding gums, bags under your eyes, etc. You may not care as much about your haircut, your clothes, your hygiene, or your grooming. The cleanliness of your uniform and equipment may not seem to matter anymore. You may also lose or gain weight rapidly—from not eating or from eating too many feel-good foods like sweets.

3. *Excessive sick leave*—Calling in sick more than is actually necessary. You may feel sick, when you're actually tired. Chronic colds, migraine headaches, and flu-like symptoms you can't seem to lick can all be stress related.

4. *Calling in sick during a shift*—Going out of service halfway through your shift, even though you might not actually be sick. This is especially a problem during graveyard shifts.

5. *Calling in sick after days off*—This leads back to the tired instead of sick effect. The stress of the job may lead you to not want to go back again. Your days off become agonizingly short, and your work week becomes way too long.

6. *A rise in citizen complaints*—This one is self-explanatory. A rapid rise in your citizen-complaint quotient tells you one thing: you're overstressed. Your supervisor will probably be the first person to point this out to you.

7. *Rapid mood changes*—In the space of a few hours or even a few minutes, you can go from happy to angry, from cheerful to uncontrollable tears. The stress you feel controls your emotions.

8. *Excessive use of alcohol or other drugs*—Needing several

beers after a shift to calm down or feel like a human being again. An overdependence on alcohol, sleeping pills, and even cigarettes may mean a stress problem. I won't even mention the use of dangerous or illegal drugs as a way to escape stress-related problems. We all know or have heard of cops who have abused drugs and subsequently ruined their careers.

9. *Sleep problems*—Sleeping excessively as a means of escape or not being able to sleep for successive nights. Chronic oversleeping or insomnia is a sign that your body is out of balance.

10. *Frequent accidents*—Auto accidents or personal-injury accidents at home or at work may tell you that your motor skills, reflexes, and balance are not sharp. Too many close calls behind the wheel of a police car or your own vehicle can also indicate a stress problem.

11. *Taking unnecessary risks*—No cover units for a major problem, trying to act like a supercop, doing things too fast or too aggressively. These examples of "tombstone courage" should point to stress problems. Obviously, this attitude can get you or another officer killed.

12. *Obsessed with the job*—Living and breathing police work, spending hours before and after your shift at the station, carrying two guns off-duty, a constant preoccupation with the job, to the extent you forsake everyone and everything else in your life. This is especially a problem with new officers who may feel defensive about their chosen career.

13. *Depression*—Tired, moody, emotional, sad, frustrated, apathetic, a feeling of heaviness. Depression can take on many forms. Chronic depression may even include suicidal thoughts.

14. *Use of excessive violence*—Using excessive force on a prisoner or a suspect, beating someone who has given up, applying pain holds beyond what is necessary. You may not even notice the symptoms, but your partner or your fellow officers do. This is often coupled with the rise in citizen complaints mentioned earlier.

These fourteen stress-related warning signs don't necessarily represent the whole spectrum of stress problems as they relate to police work, but it's a good place to begin to look at your own life and career.

Life on the streets has never been easy. You know how this job eats at you for much longer than your eight- or ten-hour shift. If you see these problems in yourself, then it's time to take steps to reduce the stress and conflicts you may be feeling. Seek out some appropriate counselors who can help you get a grip on your feelings.

For effective stress control at home, I highly recommend you get an audiotape program. You can play it before work or bed. Used regularly, a tape program can really change your stress level for the better.

A San Diego-based training company, Code 4 Products, offers the *Street-Stress Fighter* audiocassette tape. Designed and narrated by a police hypnotist, the *Street-Stress Fighter* teaches you to get control of your stress level by first learning to relax. Using the visualization techniques taught in the tape can help you get through your day with a minimum of stress and tension. For a copy, send $12.95 to Code 4 Products, P.O. Box 9292, San Diego, CA 92169.

The Tactical Retreat: Getting Out in One Piece

The title should tell you this is not an easy subject to write about. Look at it again. You say, "Okay, 'tactical' is a good start. I like tactical stuff. But what is the word 'retreat' doing in an officer safety book?"

Throughout the annals of history, dating back to jolly old England, where the first constables roamed about the countryside as the official law of the land, we've always known that police officers do not retreat. Our job is to 1) go in there, 2) kick ass, 3) take names and not back down or give up until we've finished.

On its face, this is true. We are indeed the last line of defense, the "Thin Blue Line" if you will, between good citizens and crooks. If not us, then who? But let's back up a bit.

"No way," you say to everyone in the locker room. "I don't back away from any street hoods. The word 'retreat' is not in my vocabulary."

The term "tactical retreat," as I understand it, has nothing to do with raising white flags or putting our heads in the sand like a band of frightened ostriches. First, the dictionary definition of the word "tactics" refers to "any skillful method used to gain an end." The same dictionary defines 'retreat' as "a withdrawal, as from danger."

Put them together and you get "a skillful method used to withdraw from danger." Doesn't that make sense? Now do you see where this concept can apply to police work? If not, consider these real-life examples.

Two officers working in one unit drive slowly through a high narcotics area. Suddenly, a group of ten to twelve gang members surround their car and begin rocking it and banging on the hood and roof with their fists. There is a distinct odor of ether in the air. The officers are effectively trapped in their car for a few brief moments. The driver floors the accelerator pedal and speeds away to safety. The officers regroup and call for cover units to meet them at a safe staging area. Later, they go back and make arrests. The concept of a tactical retreat worked here.

What about this scenario? A midwestern state trooper responds to an apparent accident scene. He arrives to find a lone male driver staggering drunkenly from a wrecked car. He confronts the driver and attempts to apply handcuffs. Approximately ten members of this man's family suddenly appear on the scene to "assist" him. (These people had apparently been following the drunk in two other cars.)

The trooper begins to do a five-minute version of the asphalt tango with the suspect, who is not really resisting arrest but just won't stand still. The trooper fails to use any kind of escort or pain-compliance holds to stop the suspect from walking him all around the interstate. At one point, he even drops his handcuffs on the ground. A polite teenager gives them back, and he finally succeeds in getting one cuff on the suspect's wrist.

During this entire charade, several members of the suspect's family placed themselves between the trooper and the suspect, in an attempt to "calm things down." Finally, cover units arrive, and several other troopers help to get the suspect into cuffs and away from the scene. The tactical retreat concept failed miserably here.

What saved this trooper from being disarmed and shot or beaten into unconsciousness by the crowd? His police skills? No. His command presence? No. His use of defensive tactics? No. This trooper owes his survival and, indeed, his life to the news camera crew at the scene. They began to film this entire event after witnessing the original car accident. Do you think the suspect and his family would have assaulted the officer if their actions weren't preserved forever on videotape? No doubt about it.

Would a tactical-retreat plan have saved this officer a torn uniform and several long minutes of grief? Yes. Outnumbered ten to one, the trooper was not in any position to complete the arrest. Time to disengage.

Let's go back to the first scenario with the gangsters pushing the police car. Answer these questions as you consider whether the officers did the right thing. Were they in a safe position to confront the suspects? Did they have enough officers to put the odds on their side? Were the suspects calm and rational?

Consider these other questions: Were the suspects probably high on PCP? Did the officers have to make an immediate decision as to their safety? Did they employ proper tactical retreat methods? Did they safely make the arrests later?

If you answered no to the first three questions and yes to the last four, you understand the concept of a tactical retreat.

Keep in mind that a tactical retreat has many forms. In one set of circumstances it may call for you to leave the scene altogether and in others it may just call for you to stop fighting with the suspect and loosely contain him until more help arrives.

No street situation is ever the same, but you can use certain guidelines to help your decision-making process. Remember these two rules whenever you feel you may have to make a tactical retreat: Can I take this guy? Is this worth getting killed? (The answer to this last question should always be no, regardless of the circumstances.)

If the answer to the first question is no, then you need to move on to the next step: disengage from the suspect and re-evaluate your position.

Consider these additional factors when deciding when to make a tactical retreat:

1. The suspect takes you by surprise and begins to fight.
2. You're in a bad tactical position (a freeway ramp, a crowded bar, a narrow hallway, etc.).
3. Something worse may happen if you continue.
4. The suspect gets access to a weapon or more help from other suspects.
5. You know the suspect has a violent criminal record.
6. You're badly injured or too exhausted to continue.

If any of these factors exists, it might be time to "vote with your feet" and get away from the situation.

A tactical retreat is not a sign of surrender. It is not an excuse to give up when a street scene gets too difficult. It is not a hopeless, tail-between-the-legs admission of defeat. It is, however, an alternative for your survival, and it should be a part of your survival plan during all contacts.

Ten Deadly Tactical Errors

Police officers are their own worst critics. If they see something wrong, they're quick to point it out, especially when it concerns other cops working with their guard down.

This trap is an easy one to fall into. After a few years on this job, you begin to think even the scary stuff becomes "routine." If you work in some of the busier parts of your city, a drug bust with multiple armed suspects is nearly an everyday event.

In all parts of the city, writing those FIs, tickets, and misdemeanor citations can get "routine" as well. Going to the umpteenth loud party, family fight, or boyfriend-girlfriend beef can also get "routine."

Even the dangerous stuff can feel "routine." Get the alarm ringer call, park near the scene, rattle a few doors, put out an all clear, stand around for awhile yakking, then go back in service. After your hundredth unfounded burglary call, they all start to feel "routine."

You'll note that throughout these examples of the trend toward complacency, I've put the word "routine" in quotes. I did it to make a point. *There is no such thing as a routine anything on this job.*

The point is, no matter how many times you've done it,

went to it, made it, or seen it done, each episode is different than all the rest. Complacency is a deadly disease, but fortunately, there is a cure; it's called awareness.

Way back in the academy, we all learned about the ten deadly errors for police officer survival from Pierce R. Brooks, the author of a fine book, *Officer Down, Code 3*. The list is a good one, and it bears repeating.

1. *Improper attitude*—Police work takes complete concentration. You can't perform effectively if you're distracted or preoccupied by personal problems. As hard as it is to do, you must put your problems on the so-called "back burner," so you can fully concentrate on your work. A positive, survival-based attitude is a powerful weapon for you to maintain.

2. *"Tombstone" courage*—As police officers, we're good at evaluating situations quickly and accurately. However, with the type and number of criminals we are facing today, there are few arrest situations that should be made alone. One of the best things about this job is that in most instances, you have some time to decide how to proceed. A high-risk vehicle stop is a perfect example. You don't need to pull the car over immediately after you find out it's stolen. You have the time and resources to wait for cover and properly (and safely) make the arrest. Sometimes bravery is just a mask for stupidity. Don't let any situation outnumber you. If the situation warrants it, get on the radio and get help.

3. *Sleepy or asleep*—Those hours just before sunrise on graveyards are the toughest. The urge to sleep is powerful. You need to be especially careful during these predawn hours to avoid a car accident or, worse, an ambush. Street people are very nocturnal animals. Nobody likes to be surprised by a transient standing at the car window. You need to be aware of your own body. Get the proper amount of rest, even if it means putting a limit on some of your social activities.

4. *Bad tactics or position*—Always remember to keep the suspect at a constant disadvantage. It still pains me to see officers standing next to traffic violators with their gun only a foot away. I try to treat everyone as if he or she is right-handed, so I stand positioned to ward off any right-fisted punches. Make the suspect stand in the street while you stand on the curb. Use your car, a nearby wall, or another officer as a positioning device. Use lights or the lack of light as a positioning weapon. Never give the crook the opportunity to dictate where and how the contact begins.

5. *Ignoring the danger signs*—Your intuition is another powerful weapon. Sometimes the hair on the back of your neck zooms into the air and other times it just tingles. You know when something doesn't look or feel right—maybe a whole lot, maybe just a little. It's that car with its hood up in front of the liquor store, that guy leaning against the fence across the street from the elementary school, or the car with the nervous driver. If you know your beat and your division, you should also know who "belongs" and who doesn't. Don't ignore the signs.

6. *Failure to watch suspects' hands*—This one is a given. I haven't seen anyone who can shoot a gun with his toes. Get those hands in plain sight. You are the one who controls the situation. Make them take their hands out of those pockets. Get those hands out where you can see them, even if that means up in the air.

7. *Complacency*—We've already touched on the subject of "routine" calls or stops. Be up for everything and treat every assignment as if the potential for danger is imminent. That simple traffic ticket may turn into the fight of your career.

8. *Improper handcuffing*—This one is also a given. There is no reason not to handcuff a suspect correctly. My motto is: when in doubt, cuff 'em all and sort it out later. It's much easier to take them off than it is to put them on. Good handcuffing techniques mean using approved methods and keeping the tactical advantage.

9. *Poor searching techniques*—Pay attention to your searching techniques. We have a tendency to search quickly if the previous fifty suspects weren't carrying anything more dangerous than a pocket knife. Search everyone carefully and thoroughly—even women. Sloppy searching could cost someone—like your partner, another officer, or a jail deputy—his or her life.

10. *Dirty or inoperative equipment*—This includes all of the other stuff you carry besides your gun. Your handcuffs, Mace, speedloaders, ammo, Buck knife, flashlight, and assorted leather gear should be clean, clear, sharp, and ready to use. Officers who carry semiautos should already know how to clean and care for their weapons. Officers carrying revolvers tend to let the cleanliness habit slide because the revolver is usually so dependable. I say "usually" because it only takes a speck of powder or too much oil to cause a malfunction that could end your life. Keep your duty weapon clean, and take that backup weapon out for a thorough scrubbing as well.

This top ten list should serve as a constant reminder to you. Be careful. Be aware. Don't be complacent about anything, ever.

Tombstone Courage: Tactical Errors During High-Risk Calls

The story you are about to read is true. The names have been changed to protect the lucky.

I hate to pass judgment on the actions of other officers—why steal thunder from the newspapers, who do it so often anyway? My motto has always been, "If you weren't there, you couldn't possibly know what was really going on, so you couldn't possibly make an accurate comment about the outcome."

However, in this particular incident, I was there so I believe my reactions are based upon the "intra-ocular test," or what hit me between the eyes.

First-watch shift. A priority radio call comes out: "Man with a Shotgun." The suspect is arguing with another man in a mobile home. Three units acknowledge the call and respond. I am in the third and trailing car with my partner.

As we enter the mobile home park gate, we hear a "Code 4, One In Custody" over the air. We decide to continue just to get a look at the suspect.

As I climb from my car, a gardener from the complex comes over and says, "Boy, those shotgun pellets went right by us," pointing toward his fellow workers.

"What shotgun pellets?" I say, looking toward the cuffed suspect being placed in a patrol car.

"Those," he says, pointing to a six-inch hole in the front facing corner of the suspect's mobile home.

I asked the gardener what time he heard or saw the blast and he said, "It happened right when the first cop got there, just as he was pulling up."

My mouth hung open for a bit. I got his name for the report and went to look around the suspect's house. Inside, I found another officer holding a 12-gauge shotgun and talking with a distraught male roommate. The house was in shambles and I saw more damage from the blast when it hit the thin fiberglass wall.

My partner asked the officer what happened and in essence, he related the following story, "I got here and went up to the door. I saw the guy with the shotgun and pulled my gun. I told him to put it down and we arrested him."

"Did you see the hole in the wall or hear the shot before you went inside?" queried my partner.

"No," the officer replied.

I went outside and asked the other officer what happened, and he related the following. "I got here and saw the officer on the porch with his gun out. I went up there and pulled my gun, and we arrested the guy with the shotgun."

On its face, you can say that no one was injured or killed, the officers succeeded in defusing a potentially dangerous situation, and an obviously disturbed man went to jail. But was the officer who entered the mobile home lucky or smart? *Lucky.* Did he use good officer safety tactics to approach this situation and handle it? The answer—even at the risk of angering this officer—has to be a resounding, *"No."*

Since I want this officer and every other cop to live to a ripe old age, let's look at some of the tactical errors surrounding this call.

1. *The arrival*—The officer's car was parked far too close to the suspect's house, actually within about twenty feet of the mobile home doorway. A more tactical approach would call for the officer to park a distance away and come up qui-

etly on foot to survey the scene. That includes listening carefully to the suspect's tone, demeanor, or location before making contact.

2. *The observation*—What clues might the officer have recognized? The presence and location of the shotgun pellet hole? The sound of the shot, which supposedly took place right when the officer arrived? The smell of a fired weapon? A reloading sound? Screaming? The sound of movement inside? These are all things to consider from the safety of a position of cover.

3. *The approach*. This situation had the potential to turn ugly immediately. An armed, distraught man with a shotgun, inside a house with another man. Murder-suicide? Hostage situation? Ambush of the police? The scary possibilities are nearly endless.

The officer went up the stairs alone to contact the suspect. Presumably, he knew his cover unit was "right behind him," but in this case a two-man approach is clearly essential.

Why make visual contact at all? Isn't that a good way to get your head shot off? Who knows how the room is arranged, the suspect who lives there or the officer? What alternatives could this officer have chosen besides going in? Surrounding the building with other officers and calling for the suspect to surrender?

How about Primary Response Teams or SWAT? Dramatic, yes, but maybe necessary if the suspect decided not to comply. Should we go into unfamiliar locations to meet armed crooks alone? Sorry, not me. I'll wait for my fellow troops to arrive and outnumber the crook.

4. *The arrest*. Is this a high-risk arrest? Does this arrest situation call for using all available suspect control techniques? Yes again. I didn't see or hear how the officers arrested this man, but I would certainly have employed a felony kneeling position to put the shooter in cuffs, even if he gave up, threw down the gun, and put his hands behind his back.

Again, I can only go by what I saw and what I heard from the parties involved. I mean no disrespect to the officer, and I'm very glad things turned out as they did. But you know as well as I do that this radio call could have just as easily ended in a police tragedy.

Were we lucky or smart? We were lucky. Does this type of response to an armed conflict happen often? Probably every day. Do we run the risk of losing good cops with these types of calls? Yes, and that's what makes police tactical responses so important. You can do it wrong a bunch of times and get away with it. We all know God loves police officers. But it only takes one of these armed events where you disregard the rules of good policing and die for your lack of effort. In these instances, we define "tombstone courage" as something that gets you killed.

There is always time to do it right the first time. Never assume, never guess, and never give a suspect the chance to kill you because you couldn't wait to "handle things."

Traffic Collision Investigations

Many officers tend to believe that once a report leaves their ink-stained fingers, they don't have to think about it again unless the case goes to court. Since police officers are responsible for so many different types of reports—everything from coroner's cases to stolen bicycles—it's easy to forget what happens down the line once the paperwork gets to the records division.

In my travels, I've met a variety of people whose careers relate indirectly to law enforcement. While they don't wear badges, their work depends a great deal on the quality (and quantity) of our reports. In no case is this involvement more relevant than with traffic accidents.

The list of interested parties—not just Party One and Party Two—includes insurance claim adjusters, accident investigators and reconstructors, plaintiff and defense attorneys, paralegals, body-shop owners, expert witnesses, medical doctors, and chiropractors.

I know what you're thinking. "Who cares? I just write the accident report. After I do the investigation, I just ship it over to records and let them sort it out."

Part of that is true, but the ramifications of your investigation in a typical traffic collision case go much deeper than just two cars involved in a crash. Let's follow the path of an accident and, more importantly to you, your accident report once it leaves your aluminum box.

About 9:00 P.M., Party Three (P-3) is stopped at the limit line of a traffic signal, waiting for her light to turn green. Party Two (P-2) is directly behind her, about one car length away. Party One (P-1) is in the lane behind P-2 and not paying attention to his rate of speed. He looks up to see P-2's rear bumper a few yards away. He slams on the brakes, skids for a distance, and smacks into the back of P-2's car. P-2 slides forward, and he crashes into the rear of P-3's bumper.

Each driver gets out to look at the damage and everyone agrees to pull into a nearby gas station lot to wait for the police. A station employee saw the entire accident and agrees to give a witness statement. You arrive on the scene and—after verifying that no one is injured—begin to interview the participants.

After you hear each of the four versions, you fill in the names, check the boxes, note the minor property damage, pace off the Initial Contact Points (or Points of Impact), and send everyone home.

You complete your report, finish the diagram, and turn it in for approval at the end of your shift. After an appropriate supervisor scrawls his or her name at the bottom, the report heads to records. End of story, right? Wrong. This is where the fun starts.

The next morning P-3 wakes up and notices her neck is stiff and sore. Her left shoulder is tender to the touch, and she has a slight headache. She has trouble putting on her clothes because of this stiffness. She goes out to her driveway and looks at the back of her car. She sees a good-sized dent in her rear bumper, along with some chrome damage and paint transfer. She goes into her house and makes two calls: one to her insurance company and one to a personal-injury attorney.

P-2 wakes up with the same pains in his neck and head.

He sees similar damage to his front and rear bumper, and he makes the same two phone calls to his insurance company and attorney.

P-1 feels fine except for the damage to his car. He makes one phone call: to his insurance company to tell it about his misfortune. However, in this scenario, P-1 is already in the high-risk insurance group. He's had several tickets, a few accidents, and his insurance rates are in the stratosphere. The version he tells his insurance company differs just a bit from the real truth.

In his account of the crash, the *second* car at the light hit the car ahead of him *first*, then he came along and happened to hit the back of the second car. So instead of being on the hook for two smashed cars, he's only admitting to hitting the middle one.

Parties Two and Three tell their attorneys and insurance companies exactly how the accident happened. P-2 felt two impacts; one for the initial crash and the second after he hit the car ahead of him. P-3 felt one impact when P-2 hit her from behind. But she *heard* the first crash and braced for the impact that followed.

Each attorney and each insurance company request your Traffic Collision report. Once they review it, they see the presence of Mr. Witness. Immediately, attorneys' investigators and insurance adjusters spring into action. Mr. Witness' version of the crash becomes the key to the whole case.

Everyone tracks Mr. Witness to his home and interrupts his TV time with requests for his version of the facts. He tells the same story all four times. The adjusters, the investigators, and the attorneys then get in line and hammer heavy financial blows down upon P-1 and his insurance company. Therein lies the moral to this tale: document everything on your Traffic Collision sheet. It can only help everyone involved, including you, the innocent victims, and the guilty driver.

What would be the end result of this case had you not identified the witness? Each participant will surely start a huge shouting match with each other. Accusations will fly from party to party, with each insurance company siding with its own driver. More importantly, another civilian would have the chance to bash the investigating officer and your department for "screwing up" the report.

Let's look at some of the factors you'll want to include to cover all the bases on your next traffic collision report.

- Be sure to document any complaints of pain from all parties. Stiff necks, shoulders, and backs or bruising injuries deserve mention if one or more participants say anything at all to you. Noting this information at the scene may prevent phantom injuries from appearing months after the accident.
- Try to be as accurate as possible when listing the time of the accident. Some crashes occur right at daybreak or dusk, and the use or nonuse of headlights may be a notable visibility factor for each party.
- List all available information for the drivers, including the home and business phone numbers, the races, and complete descriptions of each vehicle make, model, and type. Insurance adjusters and attorney's investigators may need to find these people literally years after the original crash.
- Use extreme care when listing insurance information for each driver. This is critical to a number of involved parties. Any laxity in recording the policy numbers and letters can cause excessive delays and extreme hardships for the drivers.
- Make sure you know if the driver actually owns the car. Verify the registration or run the plate if necessary. A large number of complicated car accident claims stem from the legal concept known as "permissive use." Put down as much information as possible about the car's owner if it's not the driver. Each insurance company will want to know who let whom drive the car and why.
- Make careful note of the vehicle dispositions. If a driver asks for a private tow, note that information in the report

to prevent any future damage claims against your municipality or its contract tow companies.

• Verify the actual posted speed limit for the street in question. Don't guess. Insurance people and attorneys have a field day when you note the wrong posted limit. It hurts your credibility as an investigator and can discredit your report.

• Similarly, try to get an accurate count of each driver's speed prior to the crash. This is another extremely sensitive point with insurance companies and lawyers. If you write "55" for the "25" posted zone, be prepared to justify this with evidence (skid marks, witnesses, damage, etc.)

• Check the whole car for damage before you color in the vehicle diagram. Be especially wary of old damage that a noncontact vehicle driver may try to pawn off as fresh. Some bad drivers get their cars fixed for free using this scam.

• Choose the appropriate damage indicator. If it's just minor damage, go ahead and check the box, but if you see signs of a badly bent frame or extreme structural damage, don't be afraid to raise your estimate of the car's condition. Noting any excessive or old damage protects you from having to guess in court years later, especially if no photos exist of the damaged car.

• Make a complete and thorough sketch, including the position of the traffic signals, the width (in feet) of the lanes, the width of the intersections—especially if they're offset—and the position of the lane dividers. Be sure to draw it out if the driver crossed a simulated island before the crash, drove in the bike lane or across construction barricades, etc. Be as precise as possible with this diagram. Use a traffic template to help you. Don't just rely on freehand drawing. You may have to testify in great detail about this intersection, and years from now it may look nothing like it did back then.

• Abbreviate as much as possible for the investigation narrative. Save space and time, but still be as clear about how the crash happened. Add any additional information at the end if it helps, e.g., "Officer Jones also witnessed the crash while off-duty across the street," or "P-1 left 100 feet of locked rear-wheel skid marks prior to impact."

• As with the driver's information, be specific about the witness information. List the sex, age, and all phone numbers for each witness. Take the extra minute to get this information right the first time. Other investigators may have to look for these people years after the crash.

• Make sure you carefully note the position and use of safety devices for all passengers and injured parties. This will prevent a nasty version of "musical chairs" later in court, where one person says *he* was in the front seat, and another person swears *he* was, with no one to corroborate either side.

• Note any vehicle defects that may have influenced the crash. No front headlights, wipers, turn signals, or a badly cracked windshield may have contributed to the accident.

• Take careful note of the weather, road conditions, and lighting at the time of the crash. Describe how heavy the fog was or how hard it was raining. Mention any obstructions in the road. This information can go a long way toward affixing the final blame for the accident later on.

• If any of the parties tells you his or her traffic signal was not working, test it and see. If the signal is damaged or broken, notify the appropriate repair facility immediately to prevent a repeat accident later. Note in your report how long you tested the signal for problems (three complete cycles, or ten minutes, etc.).

• Verify the sobriety of each driver or injured pedestrians carefully. In the excitement of the moment and in their haste to complete the report, some officers let good objective symptoms of drug or alcohol use slip by. Test carefully.

This is not new information for most veteran officers. But we all have a tendency to let some seemingly less important information fall through the cracks as we try to get everything done at a crash scene. An officer working alone may have to direct traffic, order tow trucks, assist the injured, and interview witnesses. It's hard to remember everything. Fill in all of the information you can. The more you put into the report during the investigation, the less you'll have to remember years later in court.

Traffic Direction: Rules to Live By

Police officers are called upon to direct traffic at a number of different events. It may be at an auto accident, a fire, a natural disaster, a sporting event, a traffic signal problem, or even a crime scene.

Sometimes traffic control may only require some well-placed flares and the liberal use of your hands or flashlight. Other incidents may require you to stand at a traffic post and guide cars safely for several hours. Since you can't always predict what kind of traffic scene you may be called to, it's best to be prepared for the worst.

Effective traffic direction is not something to take lightly. A critical mistake could cost the life of the approaching driver, the injured victim, bystanders, or the police, fire, and medical personnel working at the scene you're assigned to the protect. Your own life is in constant jeopardy each time you step into the path of a two-ton moving car and try to control its path.

Imagine the civil liability you'd face if you directed traffic poorly and caused another injury accident or, worse, a fatality. Once you take charge at a traffic scene, you're completely responsible for the safe passage of the oncoming cars.

Daytime traffic direction is obviously much easier than

nighttime control. During daylight hours, drivers can see you and the surrounding obstacles. Visibility is usually good enough so you can take immediate control of a scene with a minimum amount of trouble. Still, you need to take certain precautions to avoid a catastrophe.

Use your judgment when it comes to your police vehicle's lightbar. During daylight, the flashing red and blue lights may be more distracting than helpful. If you can secure the scene with just your flashing yellow lights, do so. If your lightbar is low on your vehicle, make sure you keep your trunk closed so you won't block the beams.

You'll need to decide if highway flares are needed at your daylight traffic scene as well. The design, grade, and width of the roadway, the weather conditions, and the speed limits are all areas of concern.

Flares are bright and noticeable, but there are times when their use is dangerous, like at the scene of a chemical spill or other toxic accident site. Further, you need to keep the health of your own lungs in mind as you work around flares. The smoke can be quite toxic and can cause coughing fits if you inhale it for too long. Also, the red-hot flames can burn holes in your uniform if you're not careful.

Nighttime traffic control calls for extreme caution. Unlike in daylight hours, the number of impaired drivers on the road increases dramatically. Officers are killed each year when they are run down by drivers under the influence of drugs or alcohol.

The reaction times of approaching night drivers is another area of concern. You have to arrange your traffic control scene with these time and distance factors in mind. Make sure you give drivers enough time to react safely and take the proper evasive action. Plan your approach, use some logic, and try to channel the traffic into the path of least resistance. If you need to close an entire street for a major investigation, try to set up your traffic post near alternative exits, so approaching drivers can make safe, rapid turns away from the area.

If you must direct traffic at night, take advantage of every possible source to illuminate your body. Wear an orange vest, set up cones, flashers, or pylons, wave your flashlight, use your car as a beacon, or place several flares near you to light you up to other drivers. As a side note, if you don't have an orange vest, you may want to forego that nice, warm (and black or dark blue) jacket for visibility's sake.

Monitor the life of your flares as you work. Be prepared to replace the burned ones with a fresh set. Try to do this in advance, so you don't have to leave your post to replace old flares.

A traffic direction scene is confusing to the approaching driver. We all want to look and see "what's going on." You need to give these rubber-neckers enough warning to make a safe decision to change their current path. Keep your hand signals quick and simple. Point at the lead drivers if you want them to proceed from a stop. Use your flashlight to illustrate the turning movements you want them to take.

Remember to use your whistle effectively. Short and long blasts are the key to controlling movement. Drivers are too often preoccupied with their car radios or their conversations with passengers to listen for you. Make yourself be heard.

You'll do well at traffic direction if you remember the three Golden Rules: *Be Visible, Be Careful*, and *Don't Talk*.

Rule one—be visible—is critical to your safety. Remember that every driver is not watching for you. Make yourself be seen by everybody. Lights, flares, vests, and other high-visibility devices will help.

Rule two—be careful—means you must keep your eyes and your other senses on your work. Traffic direction takes concentration. Watch the approaching traffic at all times. A number of officers can tell stories of how they had to leap out of the way of an oblivious driver. Some officers have actually jumped over their own cars to avoid being hit by another car. Never take your eyes off the traffic.

Lastly, rule three—don't talk—requires some explanation. An officer at a stadium event was trying to control traffic as it left a ball game. A woman drove past his barricades and tried to cross into the merging traffic. Instead of trying to guide the woman into the correct lane, this officer lost his sense of professionalism and cursed heatedly at her, half under his breath. Her windows were closed, but she was hearing-impaired, and she could read lips. Her complaint form was waiting for the officer when he returned to the station at the end of his shift.

Remember, don't talk, not even under your breath. Try to keep your cool and don't berate these drivers, even if they disobey your directions. Use your discretion and put yourself in the other driver's position. Make it easy for this person to get past you with a minimum of trouble, but above all, take care of your own safety first.

Working with the Feds: High-Risk Entry Safety

The beauty of this job is that it never fails to give me ideas for columns, especially when I desperately need one. I always seem to stumble upon something in the field that sets off that little "writer's bell" in my head. Riding around in a patrol car all day gives me the chance to see a variety of things that can generate officer-safety material.

My partner and I recently assisted federal agents with a dope house raid. Early one morning we drove to meet them a few blocks away from the suspect's house. We knew from a postlineup briefing with our sergeant that they were watching some heavy-duty cocaine smugglers.

My first impression as I drove up the street toward the meeting was that there were far too many guys running around in tennis shoes and windbreakers, driving up and down the street in Firebirds and Camaros and carrying many small guns in big holsters.

We listened as the team leader explained what he wanted us to do. I cringed inwardly when he told us how other neighbors spotted the agents as they staked out the suspects (by parking in front of their house).

Before we could hit the house, we had to wait for telephonic approval from a federal magistrate for several search warrants. We gave the agents a radio set on our frequency, and they gave us one from their supply.

After a few hours, one of the agents near the house reported by radio that two suspects had come out of the house and were getting into a van. As they drove up the street, we pulled our marked unit behind them, followed them to an open area, made the stop, and detained both people inside. The agents slapped on the cuffs, and our part was done.

Upon reflection, it struck me how the feds really have their own way of doing things. My partner and I noticed some tactical errors as we waited for them to get ready. After arriving on the scene, we decided to serve as backups and let them hit the house.

Everything worked out, no one was hurt, and the operation ended with suspects in custody, but the experience heightened my awareness of how we, as patrol officers, interact with federal agents in the field.

I've had other mostly positive encounters with the feds, and many patrol officers and detectives work with these people on a daily basis. But I began to think about younger officers, who may not have much experience in these interagency situations. How do you work with federal law-enforcement officers, especially during high-risk activities like search warrants?

For answers, I spoke with a narcotics street team detective, who has kicked in many a door with the federal government. The detective offered several good pieces of tactical advice.

- Protect yourself and your partners at all times.
- Work with your own partners, i.e., other cops from your own agency.
- Don't get too involved with the actual building entry.
- Volunteer to watch the perimeter or the back of the building.

- Keep an eye out for people coming up behind the agents or for other suspects in the neighborhood.
- If possible, arrange to loan the agents a radio for the duration of the arrest process and get one from them.
- Use a common frequency if you can't spare a radio.
- Use cover and concealment at all times.
- Ask for a thorough debriefing before you participate in anything. Find out who the suspects are, what they're wanted for, what types of weapons they carry, how many rooms are in the building, etc.
- If you're asked to initiate a vehicle stop, ask how and where they want you to do it, i.e., a high-risk stop on a residential street or a regular stop on the freeway.
- Don't let them talk you into doing anything you think is unsafe.
- Follow your department's approved officer-safety practices, not theirs, e.g., don't park in front of the suspect's house or handcuff suspects in front just because they do. Use the training that brings you home after every shift.

We're all cops under the skin, but sometimes the methods and practices of one law-enforcement group don't exactly mesh with those of another. Be polite, offer to help as much as you can, but be extremely careful and watch your back.

Remember that your paycheck comes from your agency, not from the Treasury or Justice Department. Your first responsibility is to yourself and your partners.

Some Final Tips

• Anticipate problems before they happen. Have a planned response ready at all times.

• Pay more attention to body language, especially the movements and mannerisms of street crooks, drunks and dopers, transients, and emotionally disturbed people.

• Practice if/then thinking at all times: "*If* he gets out of the car and starts running, *then* I will . . ."

• Practice more head shots at the range. Work on your "double-tapping" skills. Instead of "punching holes in paper," work to make each shot count.

• Maintain a safe distance, especially against armed suspects. Being close is not always the best or safest position. Twenty-one feet is the minimum distance for a suspect armed with a knife. Even a quarter mile may be too close for a suspect armed with a high-powered assault rifle.

• Move laterally away from a knife-armed suspect, not just backward.

• Pat-down carefully. Look hard for knives, box cutters, handcuff keys, nail clippers, pins, nails, lighters, needles, and razor blades.

• Look harder for weapons in vehicles—guns taped to

the roof, in the door frame, under seat cushions, inside holes in the dashboard, etc.

• Keep the suspect off-balance, both mentally and physically, whenever possible, e.g., try to make the suspect think there is more than one officer on a car stop by using lights, phantom voices, and positioning.

• Try to be well-rounded. Keep in good physical and mental condition, practice with your equipment constantly, and think tactically at all times.

• Don't do pat-downs from the "inside" position—facing the suspect.

• Monitor your own body language, especially during potentially high-risk situations. Do you exhibit a feeling of strength, control, and command presence?

• Practice controlled breathing to lower your adrenaline level during high-risk encounters.

• Don't let the suspect distract you with one hand—fishing for a wallet—while the other hand reaches for a weapon.

• Reaction is always slower than action. Act before the suspect can react. Don't let him get the drop on you.

• Watch for early warning signs that the suspect may be armed—the presence of sheaths, clips, holsters, or pouches.

• Hit hard enough to create dysfunction in the suspect—make it so his arms and/or legs don't work.

• Use distraction techniques like yelling to disorient the suspect during a fight—"Down!", "Stop!", or "Move!"

• Bring your baton everywhere and practice with it at least once per week.

• Be more careful during pat-downs; watch your gun position and keep the suspect off balance at all times.

• Contact traffic violators on the passenger side more often than you do now.

• Watch for second vehicles pulling up behind you during traffic stops. Keep the possibility of ambush in mind.

• Pay particular attention to your safety habits when working alone.

- Be particularly careful with mentally disturbed suspects.
- Think about weapons retention at all times. Keep your holster snapped until you're ready to draw your weapon.
- Practice elbow and knee strikes on a karate bag. Most suspect assaults happen in close quarters.
- Practice some kind of martial-arts movements—punches, kicks, blocks, etc.—at least three times per week. Put special emphasis on street survival situations.
- Continue to use good Contact & Cover techniques.
- Use your radio and penal codes more often when briefing other officers during Contact & Cover situations.
- Practice shooting at barricaded suspects by folding the silhouette targets in half at the range.
- Focus on officer safety during handcuffing and especially during uncuffing situations.
- Get rid of those two nice, shiny, and sharp metal pens in your front pocket. Switch to plastic pens to avoid being stabbed in a fight.
- Be careful about what you touch. Don't blindly pick up aluminum foil packages that are probably drugs, but may in fact be a booby-trapped bomb device.
- Be prepared to use a tactical retreat in high-risk situations where the odds of success are slipping.
- Search harder for knives and other edged weapons.
- Pain or the presence of blood is no barometer of how badly you are hurt. You can and will survive most gun, knife, or assault-type wounds.
- Always remember a veteran training officer's credo: God gave you hands to protect your face, a chin to protect your throat, shoulders to protect your jaw, arms to protect your body, hips to protect your groin, and, finally, a gun to protect your life.

A Last Bit of Humor: Amazingly Stupid Crooks

While there's no question police work can be incredibly frustrating, a few bright spots do emerge from time to time to thoroughly improve our outlook and help the street officer get rid of those workday blues. What follows is a list of charter members of the "Stupid Crooks Hall of Fame." For one reason or another, these men and women have distinguished themselves from their peers for their incredibly ignorant crimes. These idiots are so inept at their craft it's downright funny. For all of you cops who are beginning to lose faith in our justice system, enjoy!

1. Two convicted rapists walked away from a prison work detail in Ionia, Michigan. A farmer saw the two men trying to drain some gasoline from a storage tank on his farm. When he yelled at the men to stop, they turned and ran, apparently not seeing the twelve-foot-deep pit of liquid cow manure until it was too late. One Michigan state trooper who arrived to arrest the pair said, "I'll tell you what, they sure smelled bad."

2. A twenty-eight-year-old man from Brooklyn, New York, was hurrying to get to court to pay his $1,000 fine for a previous weapons-possession charge. A passing security

officer for the Superior Court in Brooklyn arrested him for possession of one pound of marijuana. Harry told the police he was late for court and had no safe place to stash his dope.

3. Two San Jose, California, men parked their old Cadillac across the street from an auto-parts store and walked in. One of the men distracted the salesclerk while the other grabbed a battery from a display case and fled. Police arrived to find the pair still trying to install the battery in their car. One officer called the men the "Mutt and Jeff" team. The battery, used for display only, was filled with cardboard. "We don't catch the brilliant ones," added another officer.

4. Minneapolis, Minnesota, robbery detectives had little trouble finding the man responsible for a hold-up at the Marquette Bank in the downtown area. The suspect, who left with $1,375, also forgot his wallet with two pieces of identification on the counter in front of the teller.

5. A trucker told Massachusetts State Police he had pulled to the side of the road after developing engine trouble. He said two armed men approached and hijacked his cargo. The robbers handcuffed him and unloaded his trailer of personal computers. The thieves then took him to the woods and released him. He called the police from a nearby gas station and told the arriving officers his story. The computers were later recovered from a storage center in a nearby town. Investigators arrested the trucker after discovering that he had rented the storage space.

6. One would-be "second-story" man did a poor imitation of Santa Claus after getting stuck inside a clothing store chimney. The would-be burglar wedged himself into the building's sixteen-inch chimney and spent the next eleven hours trying to free himself. His screams and his one free hand waving from the chimney top attracted passersby. Police freed the soot-covered man and took him to jail.

7. One Florida man wins the coveted "Double Stupidity" award for committing two felony ignorant acts during one

crime. He went into an Orlando bank and handed the teller a demand note that read, "Give me all your money, or else I'll shoot you. Bang!" Unfortunately, he had written the note on the back of his probation identification card. He fled the bank with a small amount of cash but was arrested minutes later while waiting for a bus next door to the police station.

8. After robbing a San Leandro, California, store, the crook decided to hide out in a house near the scene until the coast was clear. After police officers, dog patrols, and a helicopter searched the area for five hours with no luck, they pulled out and called off the search. When he thought he was finally safe, he walked out of the house with his gun and the money from the robbery. He also walked right into the hands of a police officer hiding in the bushes nearby. Said one police spokesman, "He should have made it six hours."

9. A twenty-two-year-old street hood found out the hard way why seventy-three-year-old Louise Burt is still a "tough cookie who takes no guff from nobody." Burt, a retired saleslady, was walking to a San Francisco, California, senior citizens center for a bingo game when he snatched her purse. She chased the man six blocks before two passing police officers joined the pursuit. Police had no trouble catching him after he jumped off a roof, fell two stories, and broke both of his ankles. Said Miss Burt, "He was a little shrimp of a guy, and I could have cold-cocked him with my fist right into his jaw."

10. Two female con artists in Mansfield, Ohio, tried to pull the classic "pigeon drop" on an elderly woman they met at a shopping center. They told the woman they had "found" $2,000 and said she could have an equal share if she first put up some "good faith money." They took her to her bank, where she gave them $700. Returning to the shopping center, the women gave her a "share" of the money and told her to wait for their lawyer to come by and finalize the agreement. The con artists left, no doubt happy after bilking her out of her savings. Imagine their surprise when they discovered they had given her the wrong envelope.

They had kept the packet full of shredded newspaper and given the elderly woman their original $2,000. Police decided not to pursue the case because as one officer put it, "It's not against the law to give away money."

11. Two San Diego, California, men and their partners from Tucson, Arizona, tried to steal $250,000 worth of computer equipment by paying with forged certified checks. Bank tellers noticed the poor spelling on the checks and became suspicious. The checks read "certifed," had two u's in the word "January," and spelled signature as "signture." Police arrested the men for three counts of grand theft, five counts of forgery, and one count of conspiracy.

12. A Baltimore, Maryland, robber died after shooting himself in the groin during a holdup. After the victim gave him $20, he shoved a .22 handgun into the waistband of his pants. As he backed away from the scene, the gun went off, firing a fatal round into his right groin area and piercing his femoral artery.

13. Three men robbed a Freelandville, Indiana, bank and made their getaway. Their car died about three miles away from the bank, so they called for a tow truck. The tow operator became suspicious when the men told him that "money was no object." Police arrived instead of the tow truck and recovered $10,000 and a rifle from the trio.

14. When Miami, Florida, police pulled up to help a motorist with his disabled pickup truck, they heard the driver say, "I don't know anything about the stuff in the back of the truck." Police recovered several million dollars worth of cocaine and arrested the talkative driver.

15. A well-known escaped fugitive walked into a Mexican restaurant in Ft. Lauderdale, Florida, to get a drink and a meal. Little did he know that local FBI agents were just finishing a small party in the next room. As the last agent left he spotted the crook and hurried to a phone to call his friends. Minutes later, FBI agents returned and arrested the man, who sat sipping a margarita.

16. Miami, Florida, Harbor Police chased a speedboat full

of suspected drug smugglers until it ran aground. A search of the area turned up a soaking-wet man hiding under a bush. Police failed to believe his story when he said, "I was fishing and fell off the boat and swam to shore."

17. The FBI arrested a man they had hunted for eighteen years while he was trying to get a driver's license. The suspect escaped from a Tennessee prison in 1974, while serving a life sentence for killing a police officer. He showed up at a Jacksonville, Florida, Motor Vehicles office and tried to get a new license. The state trooper on duty became suspicious when the signature on the Texas driver's license didn't match his handwriting, nor did the picture look anything like him. He tried to run but was tackled and arrested.

18. Long Beach, California, police sent local fugitives one thousand letters promising free state lottery tickets. Police officers set up an office near the Long Beach airport and answered 125 phone calls from crooks trying to find out more information. The sting operation trapped seventy-five men and women who showed up to claim their free tickets. One woman even wrote to her husband in jail to ask if she should go. He warned her that it sounded like a police trap. She went anyway and was arrested at the scene.

19. Miami, Florida, police received a call to investigate the sound of gunfire in a residential neighborhood. Two men living in a house near the scene invited the officers in to take a look around. The men apparently forgot to hide more than forty kilos of cocaine sitting on a table, along with three cardboard boxes stuffed with $1.6 million in cash. Police arrested the pair, who said they were guarding a drug-drop house.

20. A man walked into the Major Federal Savings Bank in Cincinnati, Ohio, and gave the teller six $50 bills. He asked her to change them into $100 bills. As she was changing the money, the man pulled a ski mask over his face and told her to give him all of her money. She screamed and hid behind the counter. The confused robber ran off, leaving his original $300 behind. Bank officials donated the money to charity.

21. A man held up a supermarket in Switzerland using a hypodermic syringe he said was filled with the AIDS virus. The robber left with about $2,000, but police in Bottmingen caught him later. The syringe was not filled with the AIDS virus, or any other virus for that matter.

22. Monroe, North Carolina, Police caught a burglary suspect at the scene of a wholesale jewelry store. The crook refused to speak to the officers. They waited for him to talk and when he could (literally) keep his mouth shut no longer, out popped several rings and gold chains wrapped in a rag. A police captain at the scene said the burglar had several thousand dollars worth of loot in a rag in his mouth.

23. A London, England, man was ordered to undergo psychiatric testing after being arrested and convicted of robbing local gas stations in the nude. He told the officers he didn't want to be identified by his clothes.

24. Police and fire department units in Old Bridge, New Jersey, responded to a smoke-alarm call at a home. When they came to the door, they found no fire, but rather a forty-year-old man smoking a marijuana "bong." Fire officials said the house was "filled with marijuana fumes," which had apparently set off a sophisticated smoke alarm system in the house.

25. A Pittsburgh, Pennsylvania, man was arrested for six counts of burglary. The burglar made several fatal mistakes during his crimes, beginning with the Polaroid picture he took of himself at the scene and later tossed into a nearby wastebasket. Police also found two library books he had checked out and left on a desk. They found this nitwit wandering around downtown with the Polaroid camera in his gym bag.

26. Ionia, Michigan, was the scene of a prison escape attempt. The breakout ended suddenly when the getaway car driver got lost in heavy fog and stopped to ask Ionia County Sheriff's Deputies for directions. Officers stopped the man near the Michigan Reformatory and found that his last name was the same as one of the escapees.

27. After robbing a Berlin Borough, New Jersey, bank of $1,410, three robbers jumped into their getaway car and attempted to speed away. The key word is "attempted" because the car would not get out of first gear. After an extremely slow-speed vehicle chase, they abandoned the car and tried to run. They apparently couldn't get out of first gear with their feet either, because police arrested all of them in a nearby parking lot.

28. Two bad guys in Rome, Italy, tried to rob three men by brandishing toy pistols and claiming they were police officers. The three "victims" overpowered their foes and arrested the pair for attempted robbery. The three men turned out to be police detectives investigating the murder of a prostitute.

29. Ft. Lauderdale, Florida, police are planning to teach one local crook to read "no smoking" signs more carefully. A thirty-year-old man was arrested for lighting a glass pipe full of crack cocaine while waiting in the lobby of the Ft. Lauderdale Police Department. An aid working at a complaint window spotted him lighting a glass pipe made of tubing and a small liquor bottle. The aid radioed for help, and an officer arrived to arrest the smoker, who was wearing only a pair of black pants.

30. A gang of burglars in Geneseo, Kansas, broke into the Citizens State Bank late one night and began to dig. Unfortunately, they tunneled through the wrong wall and missed the bank vault entirely. Apparently frustrated by their misfortune, the gang grabbed $50 from a teller's drawer and fled.

Not having learned from their past mistakes, the gang hit a bank in nearby Raymond. Their cutting torch set a pile of papers on fire, filling the room with smoke and aborting the burglary. One local bank president wryly observed that the gang could probably make more money robbing convenience stores.

For you foiled bank robbery fans, here are some favorit

31. One Southern California bank robber made the mistake of cutting in line at a bank he was planning to rob. An irate female customer objected to this social error and knocked him unconscious.

32. An employee of a Tulsa, Oklahoma, delivery company robbed a local bank and got away with $10,000. Trouble was that he made daily trips to that bank as a part of his job, so bank employees had no difficulty pointing him out to the police.

33. A Los Angeles, California, bank robber thought if he smeared his face with a stringent mercury solution it would make him less noticeable to the bank cameras. Unfortunately, it sharpened his features for the detectives viewing the videotapes.

34. Speaking of disguises, one bank robber dressed himself as a woman, complete with heavy makeup. In his haste to escape, he ran smack into the heavy glass doors in front of the bank. He left a nice set of "lip-prints" on the doors to convict him by.

35. FBI agents caught one down-on-his-luck bank robber at his home. He only had one leg, and he had hopped away from the crime scene with his crutch in one hand and the money in the other. Agents followed him right to his house.

36. One bank robber in San Diego, California, learned about exploding dye packets the hard way. The crook stuffed his money bag down his pants and attempted to run off. The dye packets inside these bags exploded and burned the man in a very sensitive spot.

37. A bank robber in Pittsburgh, Pennsylvania, wrote his demand note on the back of a subpoena issued in his name.

38. Another bank robber learned a lesson in timing. While attempting to rob a bank, the bad guy failed to notice the serious-looking men in the dark suits waiting in line with him. Regrettably, he chose to rob the bank during a time when several FBI agents were depositing their paychecks.

39. Bank robbery takes nerves of steel. One crook in Swansea, Massachusetts, fainted after a teller told him she

had no money to give him. He was still out cold when the police arrived. They also found his getaway car—with the keys locked inside—parked nearby.

40. Finally, one Newport, Rhode Island, bank robber canceled his own case. In his haste to escape, the nervous crook shoved his newly acquired cash into his shirt pocket and accidentally shot himself in the head. He died at the scene.

Graveyard Blues:
Riding the
Midnight Shift

If you took a random poll of patrol cops, I'd be willing to bet the ranch they would rank the graveyard shift as one of their primary career-related hardships. While certain officers will admit that graveyard hours offer more encounters with "real" crooks and less interaction with department brass, no one says he or she actually likes going to work in the dead of the night.

Besides having the chance to catch a convenience store robber, a hot prowl burglar, or maybe even a serial killer, no hard-working cop likes to work when he or she should be asleep like the rest of the world. Between 4:00 and 6:00 A.M., the human body fights for consciousness, and the urge to sleep is extremely powerful. A few officers who get into car accidents will tell investigators, "A big black dog ran across the road," rather than admit that they dozed off at the wheel.

After years of graveyard shift work, veteran officers seem to take on the appearance of vampires—blinking erratically into the noontime sun and eating their lunch at midnight. I'm convinced these hours take years off your life. Studies show that the human body functions best when it sleeps during the night and works during the day.

However, we can't ask our crooks to follow this pattern, so it's off to work we go.

• Graveyard is the time your appearance goes to hell. Dirty or wrinkled uniforms become acceptable, since you're wearing a jacket most of the time anyway. Unpolished shoes? Who cares? It's dark. If you can just get by your sergeant and into your police car, you're safe from inspecting eyes for another night.

• Graveyard hours wreak havoc on your internal body clock. If you're a male officer, your face probably looks like it always needs a shave. Graveyard hair grows at strange and mysterious rates, in strange and mysterious places.

• Bad weather can make graveyard shifts something other than a day at the beach. Heavy rains or fog beats upon your desire to get out of the car and look for crime. Of course, bad weather always seems to bring out the worst in people, so you spend your time directing traffic at accidents, answering false burglary alarms during windstorms, and talking to homeless wackos looking for a warm place to sleep.

• Your energy really starts to fade as the sun begins to peak over the horizon. From about 4:30 A.M. on, all you can do is sit in your car and hope nothing urgent or life-threatening happens on your beat. By this time of the morning, you have a bad case of "SIFLS" or "Self-Inflicted Frontal Lobotomy Syndrome." Everything you see or think about reminds you of sleep.

• If you were a righteous crook, you'd plan to do all of your capers at around 5:30 A.M. when most graveyard cops are sitting in their cars like frozen mackerels and the first watch cops are in the showers getting ready for work.

• Notice how fast everyone drives getting back to the station. Some of these cops drive faster back to the barn than they do during an actual pursuit.

• These are the same guys you find hiding out in an empty shopping center parking lot, twenty minutes before the end of the watch. Other guys hide within visual sight of the station itself, waiting for their shift supervisor to go in first.

• Going home is no picnic either. You're either so tired that you fall into microsleep at every red-light intersection, or you're so wide awake that when you get home you can't decide if you should stare at the ceiling tiles or stay up until your spouse leaves for work.

• Distractions at home include gardeners outside with ear-splitting blowers, weed wackers, lawn mowers, and hedge trimmers. These guys know exactly when you get home, and they time their workday to begin right at the moment you put your head on the pillow. I've heard of cops who actually went to motels to sleep while their homes were being remodeled.

• Unless you get at least eight hours of solid, uninterrupted shut-eye, you always seem to wake up with a tension headache that rests around the base of your skull, making it hard to move your head quickly. It feels like you have a hangover, without the benefit of having been drunk the night before.

• You're a zombie during your days off. You try to sleep normal hours with your family, but you end up watching hokey old movies on TV or telling cop stories to your cat.

• Some officers choose to work graveyards during the summer since it's mild at night. Still, this also means your bedroom can be like Dante's *Inferno* during the day. Without a sturdy fan or air conditioner at home, sleeping during the summer can be like lying on top of a barbecue.

• People want to know why we eat, stop for coffee, or write reports in local doughnut shops, thereby continuing a common police stereotype. Why? Because those places are the only businesses open late at night. We'd love to eat at Chez Snazzy but it's closed by the time we hit the field.

• Few cops have the time or inclination to brown bag their lunches, but it's not a bad idea to combat graveyard digestive troubles. Too many of those allegedly hearty breakfasts at local hash houses can make you feel like a seasick billy goat.

• Some nights there is really and truly nothing to do, so you end up padding your daily journal with scads of parking tickets written on sleepy residential streets. Imagine how happy those citizens are when they come out to go to work and find citations on their dewy windshields.

• Some nights you feel so poorly that you can conceivably come back to the station with only three entries on your journal: Left Station, Ate, Returned to Station.

Night changes the city. It brings out the worst of society. Most normal people are in bed at 3:00 A.M. The only other people out at an hour like that are milkmen and cops. Other nonpeople roaming about in the wee hours include crystal meth users fixing their transmissions, burglars, auto-theft specialists, and assorted alley "night crawlers" who peep in windows, rummage through trash cans, and howl at the moon.

If we could just convince those nonpeople to leave town, we could all get some much-needed rest.

Ten Funny Cop Stories

The very nature of police work is negative and even humorless. Few cops find time to laugh at the scene of a fatal accident, an armed robbery, an assault with a deadly weapon, or a rape. Being in the position to see the worst a city has to offer tends to wear even the toughest officer down over the years.

So what helps the street cop get through his or her working day? Simply put, it's the funny stuff about this job that makes the difference. Look back over your own law-enforcement career. Think back to the times where you went to a radio call and left with a huge smile on your face, thanks to the idiocy of some suspect, civilian, or even another cop.

I've left radio calls with tears streaming down my face because I was laughing so hard at some totally hilarious situation. They're out there, you just have to know how to find them.

Without further ado, here is a collection of some favorite cop humor stories. Each one comes from a different (anonymous) officer and tickles me in a distinct manner and will hopefully do the same for you. Best of all, each one of these street "sitcoms" is completely true. That's what makes them so good—they really happened!

• I went to this angry lizard call once. It originally came over the radio as a "Meet Reporting Party Concerning an Animal." I drove up to this large house in a residential neighborhood and found a young couple standing at the curb and looking nervously toward their house. "Can I help you?" I said as I climbed from my car.

"We called about this lizard," said the husband, who looks pretty embarrassed. "It's stuck on our door and we can't get into our house. I don't really want to touch it. It's pretty big."

Right, I thought to myself, how big can a stupid lizard be? I gave the couple my best Dudley Do-Right "stand aside, folks" look and went up to the house. They had a set of these large carved oak doors with long brass door handles. Hanging on to one of these handles was a black and green lizard that was five feet long if it was an inch. This sucker looked like a baseball bat with scales.

I studied the beast awhile and when I moved toward him he hissed, just like a cat. I decided to Mace him, so I took out my trusty spray can and gave him a blast on the head. He just looked at me, covered his eyes with his skin folds, and hissed at me again even louder. He started moving across the door, and I didn't like the way he was looking at me. I yanked out my baton and gave him a healthy whack. I squished that lizard all over those beautiful oak doors. There was lizard skin and greenish-looking blood everywhere.

When I was fairly sure he was dead, I went back to the couple and said, "Okay, folks. It's safe now. Goodnight." Lizards, brrr.

•We get this "Check the Welfare" call to assist an elderly woman. We arrived and talked to this little old lady who had locked herself out of her house. My partner boosted me up to a bathroom window, and I figured I could pop the latch. I asked the lady to get me a flat butter knife from her neighbor next door. In a few minutes she came back with a screwdriver and a cube of butter. "Will this help, Officer?"

she says as she hands me the butter. It was all I could do to keep a straight face. My partner was snickering so much he almost fell down as he was holding me up to the window.

• My very first day as a cop I went to an "Armed Robbery in Progress" call. We got to this liquor store just in time to see this very angry store owner beating the suspect with a broom. The robber got the money and ran out of the place with the owner in hot pursuit. Once he hit the street he slipped and dropped the money all over the place. People came out of nowhere to grab it. The store owner was so mad at the guy that he was really pelting him with the broom. Whack! Whack! Whack! The crook even had a gun, but this store owner was just beating the stuffing out of him. I never saw a bad guy so happy to see the cops. We saved him from a real whipping.

• I went to a noninjury accident call one afternoon. The cars were parked in the street, so once I'd determined the crash point, I asked the drivers to move their cars. The first guy gets into his car and moves it over to the curb. I guess the second driver was still a bit upset over the accident. He got into his car and proceeded to hit two parked cars as he tried to bring his car over to the side of the road. I just stood there with my mouth hanging open in amazement.

• I had this crazy partner once. We were working on the Fourth of July, and we had confiscated dozens of firecrackers. As I drove back to the station at the end of shift, this nut was lighting the firecrackers and throwing them at my feet. He kept lighting them and laughing like a maniac. He lit one and threw it at me again. I picked it up and threw it back at him. He didn't know what to do with it, so he put it in the glove compartment, not remembering all of his tickets and reports were in there. BANG! He opened the glove box to find all of his paperwork in flames. When we got back to the station, he spent the next four hours rewriting everything.

• I had a lot of glue-sniffers on my beat. I used to catch them down by the riverbed, sniffing glue-soaked socks in paper bags. One day, I saw this group of twelve-year-olds passing a bag around. Each kid would open the bag, stick his head in, quickly close it, and hand it to another kid who did the same. I snuck up on the little crooks and grabbed them by the necks. I took the bag from one of them and shoved my hand inside. About five lizards jumped out and ran up my arm. To say I was a bit surprised would be an understatement. The kids were really mad at me for letting their scaly pals get away.

• I drove on my first night on the job. We were on the freeway, and my partner pointed to a set of taillights that was really moving out ahead of us. I got excited and floored the car. I was racing up the freeway really trying to catch this guy. My partner was yelling, "Don't let him get away!" I couldn't see the car because we were so far away but I was yelling into the radio about where I was and what I was doing. I started to gain on the guy when he suddenly pulled over. When I caught up to him, I realized I'd been had. It was another patrol car. Those guys laughed at me for three days.

• I don't suffer practical jokes too well. My first week at this new station, one of the old veterans thought it would be funny to lock me in a holding cell with a bunch of weekend drunks. He grabbed me and threw me in there for about forty-five minutes. I had locked my gun and baton in the locker next to the cell. When someone finally let me out, I went straight outside and snuck over to this guy's car. I sprayed an entire canister of Mace into his air conditioner. It happened to be about 100°F that day. He laughed at me and got into his car to leave. He drove off, flipped on the air conditioner, and got a whole faceful. He hit several patrol cars before he could get control. He got one day off for messing with me, and I got three days, but it was worth it.

• My partner and I were eating hot dogs at this fast-food place when a pursuit call came out. I threw the car in gear and drove off. We caught up to the suspect's vehicle a few blocks away and closed in on him. When he stopped, we drew our guns and jumped out. I yelled for him to stop and realized I was pointing my hot dog and my gun at him. Good thing he gave up anyway.

• I consider myself to be an intelligent adult. So why is it that I have so much trouble operating a motor vehicle while dealing with any kind of drinkable liquid? One cold winter night I sat in my car drinking coffee. A robbery call came out one block away, and I wanted to zip over to it. I started the car, floored it, and tore off down the street. The coffee was sloshing all over my hand, so I decided to toss it out. Big mistake. I forgot that I had closed the window a few minutes earlier. The coffee bounced against the glass and then all over my face.

In the summer, I like to drive around with a cold drink in a rack fastened to my lightbar control panel. En route to a hot call, I went around a sharp corner quite fast. The top popped off of the cup and thirty-two beautiful ounces showered over me like holy water.

Another time, I was driving down a dark street at high speed. I didn't see any signs for anything, so I missed the huge dip in the road. I hit that sucker so hard that I whacked my head on the ceiling of the car and spilled the full can of soda between my legs. You can guess how that looked when I went to my next call.

▼　▼　▼　▼　▼

So there you have it. These brief stories are just a sampling of what goes on out there. Laughter is good medicine, so lighten up and enjoy yourself out there.

Why Do We Put Up with You? A View from the Supervisor

Since I know the brass has its own list of gripes, and it's probably as long or longer than the one carried around by the average patrol officer, I now present twenty-five items—for the brass and in no particular semblance of order—that come from a file that I call, "Did you ever notice . . . "

• When the captain comes to inspect your squad, they always look like a band of refugees, even if you've given them one week's notice concerning his arrival. (One guy looks like he slept in his uniform three nights running, and his partner has to blow the cobwebs out of his gun barrel.)

• The deputy chief always comes down to the station when you look the least efficient. Things are in an uproar, the phones are ringing off the hook, no one seems to be doing his or her job too well, and you're wearing the one tie that doesn't go with your white shirt and gray slacks.

• You always seem to get called into the field thirty seconds after you've sat down with a hot cup of coffee and a bagel. When you return, the coffee is tepid, and the bagel is quietly digesting in someone else's stomach.

• Whatever end of the division you happen to be in, you

can bet on getting a call from one of your troops clear on the other side of town. (By the time you get there, the need for you has passed because some other supervisor came by and handled the whole thing.)

• Why do old drunks in the park look at your sergeant stripes and still call you "corporal?"

• When you have minimum staffing, the crap hits the fan all over town. When you have maximum staffing, your guys sit around all night with nothing do.

• The worst command decision of your supervisory career (letting the Lindbergh baby killer go free, etc.) is captured for eternity on the nightly news.

• Commanding officers' meetings seem to take maximum time and provide minimum accomplishment.

• The guy who couldn't get out of his own way in the academy, who wouldn't know a felony arrest if it landed in the seat next to him and can't write three sentences without using an eraser, makes rank before you do.

• In a few years, this same idiot makes it to the chief's office, even though you've got more time in court than he has behind the wheel of a patrol car.

• The guy who treated you like dirt when he was your sergeant now tries to act like old buddies when you make rank.

• Whenever you get to a scene requiring some important piece of supervisory equipment (bullhorn, crime-scene tape, a capture net, etc.), you probably don't have it because the last guy to use your car broke it, lost it, or forgot to replace it.

• The suspect who acts like a complete jerk in front of one of your troops suddenly becomes the Mr. Politeness Poster Child when you appear with stripes or bars on your uniform.

• As a supervisor, the buck stops with you. This has its drawbacks: so goes the screw-ups, so goes the blame. But it also has its advantages because you call the shots and it's your reputation and success rate on the line, not anyone else's.

• The officer you give the Safe Driving Award to hits

your personal car as he leaves the parking lot.

• You feel like you're stuck with all of the paperwork and all of the responsibility. Your troops feel like they're stuck with all of the paperwork and all of the responsibility because you don't spend as much time in the field as they do.

• How fun it is to drive up to the scene, make a command decision, then drive like a bat out of hell back to the station, and sit in your warm office for the rest of the night.

• How fun it is to assign your squad's "problem child" to the worst details and the crummiest beats just out of spite.

• How fun it is to drive around in a car with "Supervisor" marked on the side.

• The quantity of your paperwork is far more important than the quality. The big guys uptown want reams from you, and they don't particularly care what it's about as long as it's on time.

• Getting "bumped uptown" removes you from all your friends. They're still around, but you just don't get together as often as you should.

• On some squads, it always gets deathly quiet when you pass through the troops' locker room. They could all be laughing at the funniest joke ever told, but as soon as your head appears in the doorway, the noise level grinds to a halt.

• Things in the field always go to hell three minutes after you've taken off your uniform. Then you have to decide if you want to dress again and go handle it or let another supervisor respond. (You usually get dressed and go because you hate to miss out on the action.)

• Getting promoted does little to help your dry-cleaning bill. Before it was $15 a week on uniforms; now it's $25 a week on dress shirts, ties, and pants.

• The neat and clean staffing schedule you've just typed up is suddenly ruined by four officers who either call in sick, take the day off, oversleep, or get in an accident on the way to work.

There you have it: twenty-five reasons why your position in the hot seat is tremendously enjoyable (although it's no bed of roses). But all things considered, would you trade those stripes, those bars, or that gold shield for anything in the world? Not on your life.

Why Do We Do What We Do? A View from Patrol

While there is certainly no such thing as a routine radio call or a routine traffic stop, there are some absolute routines in law enforcement. For better or for worse and like it or not, certain events in the field happen over and over again.

In no particular order, here are a few things about police work that also come from my "Did you ever notice . . ." file.

• Every motorcyclist these days thinks he's Mr. Ninja Rider or Tom Cruise from the movie *Top Gun*. When you stop him after a high-speed chase, he always says, "Who me?"

• You always nab the worst drunk driver at the end of the shift. This guy is so juiced he needs training wheels just to stand up.

• The last Field Interview of the night—spotted fifteen minutes before you're supposed to go in—has at least five bookable warrants.

• The most complicated report of your career—the robbery/kidnapping/auto-theft caper—always comes about one hour before the end of your shift. (You hear only dead silence on the air when the dispatcher asks for another officer to assist you.)

• Your beat car is the only one in the city that has a

heater that doesn't work in the winter and an air conditioner that doesn't work in the summer. Or, if you're really lucky, in the summer, the heater comes on when you turn on the air conditioner and, in the winter, the air conditioner comes on when you put on the heater. This usually coincides with the days you wear a longsleeve uniform shirt or forget your big jacket.

• The gas pumps always break down when you pull your car up to them. (You're usually at the beginning of a line of about eight cars, each with less than one-quarter tank left.)

• The combative prisoner always turns into an angel once he sees those big jailhouse doors swing open. You were hoping that he would irritate the deputies and receive some special treatment, but it doesn't happen.

• Every single time you're late to roll call, your sergeant is early, or the captain is there and he's early too.

• You always have the most outdated mapbook when it comes to finding a new street (which you usually must get to in a major league hurry).

• Cover calls are always on streets you either have never heard of, have never been to, or are traveling on the opposite side of on the freeway.

• You always say or do something stupid (or career-threatening) when the television cameras are at the scene.

• You can polish your shoes and clean your gun for weeks without ever facing an inspection. The one time it looks like you polished your shoes with a wet chocolate bar, or your gun is full of "holster feathers" after a trip to the range, you have a major inspection, conducted by the one sergeant in your division who thinks you're a goof-off.

• You never get into a police-equipment accident in a junky old beat car, only one of those brand-new beauties with about forty-one miles on the odometer. If you're really blessed, you get into this accident only days after receiving a "Safe Driving" award from the captain.

• You always spill Saturday night Chicken McNugget

sauce on the uniform you just picked up from the closed-on-Sunday cleaners.

• The greasiest, smelliest transient always picks your car, your uniform, or your shoes to throw up on. This clown could aim himself directly at your partner and still hit you with debris.

• During football season, you work second shift hours with weekdays off. You have great days off during hockey season, which is fine, except you hate hockey.

• Your days off or hours never coincide with the Super Bowl, the NCAA Final Four, any game of the World Series, or any NBA playoff game.

• When you go to graveyard hours, every single one of your beer buddies goes to daywatch hours. They spend a good deal of time telling you what fun they all had the previous night while you were at work.

• Crooks—who watch far too many episodes of "Miami Vice" and never practice—can shoot like Buffalo Bill, while some of us can't hit a fixed paper target at seven yards, using a seventeen-shot semiauto, without Divine Guidance.

• If it's any kind of new piece of equipment (radio, light bar, first-aid kit, etc.), it immediately breaks or gets broken. If it's an old piece of equipment and it works, it disappears. (When and if it ever turns up again, it's broken, and somebody thinks it's your fault.)

• The legal update material you missed at a previous roll call covered some incredibly obscure point of law that is a major part of the case you now have to make an arrest for.

• When you have something important to do after your shift (a hot date, a ball game, or a family gathering), you can always expect to work at least enough overtime to make all waiting parties very angry. You can also expect them to think it's your fault for dawdling at work.

• The lights-and-siren idiot who argues, screams, and yells about not signing his ticket because he "didn't do anything" usually signs it within the first twenty seconds after the supervisor arrives, thereby making you look like you can't do your job. Thankfully, if he ever shows up in court to fight the cite, the judge doubles his fine out of spite.

• The people who complain longest and loudest about police brutality usually complain even louder when we didn't get there fast enough to prevent their houses from being burglarized. Fortunately, these people become true believers when you catch the crooks and recover their property.

I only picked the top twenty-four anecdotes that came to mind. You can surely think of at least twenty-four more that are equally frustrating, funny, or mind-boggling. If most people had to put up with all of these problems and hassles, they'd quit their jobs in a New York minute. Congratulate yourself on your ability to stick it out and get your work done.

About the
Author

Steve Albrecht is nationally known for his written work on officer safety and tactics. He has been with the San Diego Police Department since 1984, both as a regular officer and now as a reserve. He is a member of the American Society of Law Enforcement Trainers and contributes articles to police publications across the country. He co-wrote *Contact & Cover: Two-Officer Suspect Control* with John Morrison.